The Authorities

Powerful Wisdom from Leaders in the Field

CHERYL IVANISKI D.Ac., C.H., RDH

*Bestselling Quilly & Global Award Winning Author, Speaker,
Dr. Holistic Medicine - Dr. Acupuncture, Health Authority,
Founder: Lifestyle Wellness Centre & Diabetes Wellness Centre*

Copyright © 2018 Authorities Press

ISBN: 978-1-77277-243-2

All rights reserved. No portion of this book may be reproduced mechanically, electronically, or by any other means, including photocopying, without permission of the publisher or author except in the case of brief quotations embodied in critical articles and reviews. It is illegal to copy this book, post it to a website, or distribute it by any other means without permission from the publisher or author.

Limits of Liability and Disclaimer of Warranty

The author and publisher shall not be liable for your misuse of the enclosed material. This book is strictly for informational and educational purposes.

Warning – Disclaimer

The purpose of this book is to educate and entertain. The author and/or publisher do not guarantee that anyone following these techniques, suggestions, tips, ideas, or strategies will become successful. The author and/or publisher shall have neither liability nor responsibility to anyone with respect to any loss or damage caused, or alleged to be caused, directly or indirectly by the information contained in this book.

Medical Disclaimer

The medical or health information in this book is provided as an information resource only, and is not to be used or relied on for any diagnostic or treatment purposes. This information is not intended to be patient education, does not create any patient-physician relationship, and should not be used as a substitute for professional diagnosis and treatment.

Publisher
Authorities Press
Markham, ON
Canada

Printed in the United States and Canada.

FOREWORD

Experts are to be admired for their knowledge, but they often remain unrecognized by the general public because they save their information and insights for paying customers and clients. There are many experts in a given field, but their impact is limited to the handful of people with whom they work.

Unlike experts, authorities share their knowledge and expertise far more broadly, so they make a big impact on the world. Authorities become known and admired as leading experts and, as such, typically do very well economically and professionally. Most authorities are also mature enough to know that part of the joy of monetary success is the accompanying moral and spiritual obligation to give back.

Many people want to learn and work with well-respected and generous authorities, but don't always know where to find them. They may be known to their peers, or within a specific community, but have not had the opportunity to reach a wider audience. At one time, they might have submitted a proposal to the For Dummies or Chicken Soup for the Soul series of books, but it's now almost impossible to get accepted as a new author in such branded book series.

It is more than fitting that Raymond Aaron, an internationally known and respected authority in his own right, would be the one to recognize the need for a new venue in which authorities could share their considerable knowledge with readers everywhere. As the only author ever to be included in both of the book series mentioned above, Raymond has had the opportunity to give back and he understands how crucial it is for authorities to have a platform from which to share their expertise.

I have known and worked with Raymond for a number of years and consider him a valued friend and talented coach. He knows how to spot talented and knowledgeable people and he desires to see them prosper. Over the years, success coaching and speaking engagements around the world have made it possible for Raymond to meet many of these talented authorities. He recognizes and relates to their passion and enthusiasm for what they do, as well as their desire to share what they know. He tells me that's why he created this new nonfiction branded book series, The Authorities.

Dr. Nido Qubein
President, High Point University

TABLE OF CONTENTS

Introduction V

The Healthy Entrepreneur 1
Cheryl Ivaniski D.Ac, C.H., RDH

Step Into Greatness 15
Les Brown

Branding Small Business 25
Raymond Aaron

Sex, Love and Relationships 37
Dr. John Gray

Never Give Up! My Journey to Purpose 43
Vivian Stark

Simple Steps for Big Results in Boosting Heart Health 61
Ralston Powell

Break Free From Your Pain Cycle 73
Seema Giri

The Modern Healer 101
Herman Siu and Martin Siu

The Love Drug 119
Wilma David Aguila

Nobody Got Time For That! 141
Ursula Garrett

Coping With Cancer 159
Yvonne Abou-Nader

Bringing Balance to Your Life 177
Dennis Garrido

INTRODUCTION

This book introduces you to *The Authorities* — individuals who have distinguished themselves in life and in business. Authorities make a big impact on the world. Authorities are leaders in their chosen fields. Authorities typically do very well financially, and are evolved enough to know that part of the joy of monetary success is the accompanying social, moral and spiritual obligation to give back.

Authorities are not just outstanding. They are also *known* to be outstanding.

This additional element begins to explain the difference between two strategic business and life concepts — one that seems great, but isn't, and the other that fills in the essential missing gap of the first.

The first concept is "the expert."

What is an expert? The real definition is …

EXPERT: *a person who knows stuff*

People who have attained a very senior academic degree (like a PhD or an MD) definitely know stuff. People who read voraciously and retain what they read definitely know stuff. Unfortunately, just because you know stuff does not mean that anyone respects the fact that you do. Even though some experts are successful, alas, most are not — because knowing stuff is not enough.

Well, then, what is the missing piece?

What the expert lacks, "the authority" has. The authority both knows stuff and is *known* to know stuff. So, more simply …

AUTHORITY: *a person who is known as an expert*

The difference is not subtle. The difference is not merely semantic. The difference is enormous.

When it comes to this subject, there are actually three categories in which people fall:

- People who don't know much and are unsuccessful in life and in business. Most people fall in this category.

- People who know stuff, but still don't leave much of a footprint in the world. There are a lot of people like this.

- Experts who are also *known* as experts become authorities and authorities are always wondrously successful. Authorities are able to contribute more to humanity through both their chosen work and their giving back.

This book is about the highest category, *The Authorities* — people who have reached the peak in their field and are known as such.

As you read this book, you will recognize many well-known names, and learn from their expertise. Cheryl Ivaniski is no exception. Cheryl is a wellness authority and recipient of the Quilly Award, which was presented to her on the Red Carpet in Los Angeles, California. This is a most honourable award for a Best-Selling Author. She is a member of the National Academy of Best-Selling Authors and the National Association of Experts, Writers and Speakers. Cheryl joins world thought leaders including Jack Canfield, who she has joined at world thought leading summits and who interviewed her for Hollywood Live TV. She also appears on networks including ABC, CBS, NBC, and FOX. She has been featured in leading magazines including the Canadian Real Estate Wealth (Crew) Magazine, and Women's Millionaire. She has written books with 5 of the World's Top Thought Leaders and Motivational Speakers, including Jack Canfield, Brian Tracy, Les Brown, Dr. John Gray,

Raymond Aaron, as well as the World Organization of Natural Medicine. She is a successful businesswoman and has been a coach to thousands of professionals, entrepreneurs, business clients and individuals.

She is a life-long entrepreneur who understands what stress can do to the body. After a near-death experience that left her comatose, with only a trace of life in her body, she realized that, if she was going to have any quality of life, she needed to take 100 percent responsibility for her health and wellbeing. Rather than reacting to her circumstances, she began embracing a new and heightened awareness, realizing there is so much more. In fact, a whole new world of more. Cheryl grew beyond traditional medicine, inviting into her life every healing art and practice that she could find, or that found her.

Cheryl comes from an authentic place of inspiration, healing and hope. Cheryl combines the best of traditional and naturopathic medicine, and believes true healing occurs when we are connected with our higher self.

As a life-long learner, she is always advancing towards the next level in balancing work, home and rest. She is a visionary who stands for people living a complication-free and disease-free, vibrant life. She founded 'The Lifestyle Wellness Centre' and 'The Diabetes Wellness Centre,' where she is helping people just like you to prevent, repair, and reverse the complications of diabetes and pre-diabetes with coaching programs, workshops, and retreats.

Cheryl believes that living a healthy lifestyle includes having a healthy relationship with money, finances, and income. Financial freedom reduces stress and offers a whole new world of choices and enriching life experiences. As a professional coach, real estate investor, and multiple franchise investor/owner, Cheryl thrives on mentoring others in living healthier and wealthier lives. Now she wants to help you live your life to the fullest.

Her chapter is all about how she finds solutions to everyday stresses to enrich her quality of life, allowing her to have the time and freedom to enjoy it. She shares how you can diffuse stress, and even overcome stress and not let it rob you of life like it almost did to her. She shares practical tips that you can use to decrease stress in your life and live a vibrantly well life. Visit: LifestyleWellnessCentre.com, DiabetesWellnessCentre.com

They are *The Authorities*. Learn from them. Connect with them. Let them uplift you. Learning from them and working with them is the secret ingredient for success which may well allow you to rise to the level of Authority soon.

To be considered for inclusion in a subsequent edition of *The Authorities*, register to attend a future event at www.aaron.com/events where you will be interviewed and considered.

The Healthy Entrepreneur

Claim Your Power, and Kick Stress to the Curb

CHERYL IVANISKI
D.Ac., C.H., RDH

"Stress is from Fear.
Freedom from Stress is your Divine Right
You have the Power to Heal your Life.
We always have the Power of Our Minds…
Claim and Consciously use your Power."

– Louise Hay

Have you ever experienced so much overwhelm that your body got so stressed that you thought it was going to shut down? If you have, then we have something in common … so read on.

Being raised on an organic farm with homegrown vegetables, fruits from orchards, and free-range animals, including chickens, pigs, cows, and goats, everyone in my family was a healthy eater, very hard-working, and very physically active. Growing up with these qualities, I was always a perfect weight and height. I thought I was invincible. I was on the go, go, go, just like my parents and grandparents.

Being a super-active entrepreneur, I not only was an independent practitioner, I founded my first educational consulting firm for doctors, dentists and health professionals. I built my business in my 20's, authoring over 30 modules of post-graduate education, and travelling throughout the USA and Canada, training sales teams and college professors, and coaching teams of dentists, hygienists, and support staff with my leading edge massive coaching programs. Then I abruptly learned I was not as invincible as I thought.

You can imagine the shock to me when, while delivering a presentation at the Annual Dental Association Conference at the Toronto Convention Centre to a group of dentists, doctors and health professionals, I felt the experience of the ceiling falling on me and the stage swirling up from under me.

Staggering to my booth, I fell into a comatose state and was immediately rushed to the hospital. My blood sugars exceeded the highest number recordable. I was in and out of consciousness with severe abdominal pain, severe dehydration (even though I was drinking tons of water, my cells simply did not absorb it), and lethargy beyond belief.

Not only was I in extreme distress health-wise, but my grandmother was dying from the complications of diabetes at this time as well. I had never lost a loved one before, so this was emotionally devastating to me. After 6 months of lingering pain in my tooth and no relief from multiple root canal surgeries, I learned that a hairline fracture was the cause of this stressful pain and that oral surgery (extraction) was my only remedy. Not only that, scabies was rampant in the community living centre where Grandma moved to, and as contagious as this is, I got this to. This added great stress on my body. In addition, while I was recovering and adapting to my new way of life, one of my trainers in my business had stolen my 30+ training modules of copyrighted education, and used them as her own for her own gain. Then the multiple lawsuits began.

All these experiences occurring simultaneously was beyond stressful; they were extreme, blowing out not one but two life-giving organs and glands. I can tell you from experience that I understand STRESS.

With these many stresses at one time, my body was overtaxed, severely overstressed, and trying to cope with way too many things at once.

Not only did my pancreas blow out and stop working altogether (resulting in type 1 diabetes), but my thyroid did too. Both are life-threatening, and they happened at the same time— a double whammy.

I was in and out of consciousness, and lucky to be alive. I was told both my pancreas and my thyroid gland would not recover (as in never work again,) and I would need to give myself multiple daily injections of insulin (5-9 per day) in order to stay alive. I would also need to take oral medications for the rest of my life to treat Hashimotos Thyroiditis. If you have diabetes and/or underactive thyroid issues you know how your body tires and then just stops. My mind could keep going; in fact it never stopped, but my body would simply tire out. The feeling is like when your cell phone battery is on its last 5 percent of charge and then eventually it needs to recharge or it just stops working altogether. It is a panic. We must recharge, rebalance and be mindful and kind to ourselves all day long, because we are not cell phones with batteries. We have one body and one life.

WHAT IT TOOK TO GET MY ATTENTION

It is important to note that I had not been feeling my energetic self for weeks. I called my doctor because I was so concerned, something I would not normally do. I said to him, "I am beyond exhausted and something is not right; I can feel it." I had never been tired before, ever!

Because my doctor has known me for over 10 years and knows that I am a workaholic, he said, "You are overworking yourself, so just take a break." He initially blew it off, but then heard something in my voice. He asked me what I thought it was. I mentioned I thought it was really serious because I had a huge appetite, which was rare, and at the same time I had lost over 20 pounds in the previous 2 weeks. He said to come in the following week and he would do blood work and a complete exam. By that time, my body was already shutting down.

THE SIGNS OF STRESS

My body had been speaking to me for quite a while, but I was on overdrive and I didn't realize how serious all the signs were. I was young, had lots of energy +++, good DNA, a great attitude, and a full life ahead of me. I had no clue of what was going to happen next. This is very common for people who do not act on these signs and give attention to the big and small things that are happening in their body. Why? Because it seems there are much bigger things to focus on. But there is nothing more important than your health.

I encourage you to read this list of the signs of stress carefully. Some are obvious, but others you may not know about. If you see yourself in this list, it is time for a reality check. It is time to look at your life and make some changes before your body forces you to make changes. So many people don't find out that they have a health concern or diabetes, no matter what type it is, until they feel pain, have a heart attack, have a leg amputated, kidneys that are failing, or they start going blind. Do not let that be you.

Agitation

You become easily agitated because stress affects your mental and cognitive ability. There can be confusion, memory loss, and the inability to focus. Instead of resting to get back focus, you consume coffee, alcohol, or comfort food to provide temporary relief. Then you get right back to work.

Skin Irritation and Pain

Whether it's acne, a rash, or itchy skin, these types of things can affect a body that is overstressed. The other physical thing that shows up for people is pain. I suffered 24 years with migraine headaches. Whether it is a tension headache, a migraine, back pain, or any continual pain in the body, it needs to be addressed, and you need to be aware that your body is talking to you. These are all warning signs.

Stomach and Digestive Issues

Intestinal issues, cramps, heartburn, and constipation are also signs of stress. Because digestion is such a big area, affecting millions of people, and many books are written on this subject, my goal is that you become aware that your body is talking to you.

Oral Issues

As a registered dental hygienist, clinical professor, and CEO of my dental educational consulting and coaching firm for over 20 years, I saw all types of stress in the mouth. Hygienists provide therapy for clients with gum disease all day long. Bleeding gums and gum disease, called periodontal disease, are warning signs and strongly correlated with immune system challenges, including diabetes and heart disease.

Fatigue

If you are habitually tired, lack in stamina, and often feel that you don't have any more energy left, your body is telling you that you are overstressed. I remember feeling like all I wanted was to keep doing, doing, doing and going, going, going, but sometimes I was just too tired. I had never, ever experienced being tired, so this was devastating. Now I realize that the best thing to do is to honour your body and to serve your body because you only have one, and it needs rest.

You are not invincible. Sleep and restful naps are the times when your body has the opportunity to repair and regenerate. Interfering with your body's ability to repair causes many chronic diseases, including immune system challenges such as diabetes. My grandpa lived to be 100 years young, and very healthy. One of his secrets to living a long healthy life was napping each afternoon after lunch for 30-40 minutes.

Weight Gain

The other thing that shows up with a lot of people, and this is something that I had experienced over time as well, is weight gain due to a hormonal imbalance. This imbalance takes place when you are overstressed because your body is in a constant state of fight or flight. This results in excess cortisol production which, in turn, causes your body to deposit and store fat. It is worth noting that this is also a sign of a challenged underactive thyroid or a condition known as Syndrome X. This affects 85% of those with type

2 diabetes, and one in six people, which is at least 32% of the American population, according to the American Heart Association.

Mental and Sleep Issues

Depression, mood swings, changes in appetite, sleep problems, and a decreased libido all may be attributed to stress.

When you cannot sleep well due to stress and anxiety, you are at risk of having a panic attack. Anxiety, depression, and other emotional issues affect your quality of sleep, which in turn affects your health and your ability to heal.

Increased Alcohol and Drug Use

When people are stressed, some use alcohol, prescription drugs, or recreational drugs for relief and release. Some people turn to food as comfort, to relieve how they are feeling.

Instead of working through stressful issues, people use these substances and other habits to treat their internal pain. Often, people become reliant on these substances to help them make it through the day.

Therefore, be careful that you are not starting to crave these substances, as that could indicate a symptom of stress and addiction.

If one or more of the items on this list resonate with you, it could be a good time to look at your life and assess where you really are. You may think that your big goals are worth the sacrifice, but if you destroy your body getting there, how will you enjoy it? I am here to say, it is not worth it.

6 SIMPLE PRINCIPLES ON HOW TO DESTRESS

I have good news for you. Decreasing stress in your life does not have to be hard or time-consuming. You do, however, need to make a conscious choice to be mindful of your body, and plan times in your day to destress. Let's take a look at six simple principles to lessen the stress in your life and get more done in your day.

For free exercises to help you relax and let go of mind chatter, anxiety, and stress, go to www.lifestylewellnesscentre.com and diabeteswellnesscentre.com.

Quality of Sleep

One of the biggest stresses on the body is a lack of quality sleep. If you look at how many hours the average person gets, compared to what they need, you'll notice a big difference. Adults need, on average, seven hours, and as you get older you need a little bit more. However, very few people get this much sleep.

We need an adequate amount of sleep so that the body can repair itself. Sleep is the time when the body recovers from the day of stresses. Sleeping is not just about repairing and rejuvenating, it also gives you an energy reserve so that you are good for the next day and the days to come.

One thing that helps you get a good night's sleep is a bedtime routine. Preparing yourself for a good quality night of sleep means going to bed around the same time each night. Here are some things you can do to help relax yourself and get ready to sleep.

- Epsom salt bath
- Essential oil bath (eucalyptus, black pepper, orange, tangerine, lavender, chamomile, etc.)

- Essential oils in a diffuser, on a pillow, rubbed into the body (temples, wrists, under nose, neck and shoulders, and bottom of feet)

- Take the recommended levels of good quality magnesium and calcium, and possibly increase the dosage, depending on brand and body absorption rates

- Melatonin – a natural sleep aid

- Non-caffeinated herbal teas or warm water with apple cider vinegar or lemon and lime

It doesn't matter what your routine is. Maybe you like to read, meditate, or listen to soothing music. The essential thing is to find what works for you and do it daily. Having an inviting and conducive space to rest is key. Having a space that is free of cell phones, tablets, computers, and other electronics that contribute to damaging electro smog that keeps your mind wired is a must.

Ease Time

Ease time is chill time. I like to think of it as my personal time. People like Jack Canfield, Oprah Winfrey, Elon Musk, Craig Newmark (founder of Craigslist), and other top performers talk about what they do in their day and refer to their power hour of the day. They talk about it in their speaking engagements, books, interviews, etc.

When it comes to meditation, what relaxes you and makes you feel most comfortable is what is right for you. It could be a morning meditation with music or in quietness, it could be inside the comfort of your own home, or it could be outside in nature. Meditation is for you personally. It's about spending time with yourself and doing things that allow your mind to be free and relax.

I know some people who just love the Beatles, Bob Seger, the Eagles, and instrumental music that helps them relax their mind. Others enjoy a hobby like playing the piano or guitar, reading, biking, gardening, painting, building things of wood – carpentry, etc. Whatever it takes, you need to find what is good for you.

You need to plan it into your day, or it will not happen. Make it a priority. For many people that means getting up earlier in the day. It also does not have to be every day. Three times a week is sufficient; however, establishing a daily routine is something I strongly recommend. The other essential thing to understand is that it does not have to be in an hour block. You can split it up in whatever way works for you throughout the day.

For free journal pages and to learn more about how to reclaim more time for yourself, please visit: www.lifestylewellnesscentre.com or www.diabeteswellnesscentre.com.

Rejuvenation Break

Why should you take a rejuvenation break? When you are doing the same thing all the time, your mind and body need an interruption to keep them stimulated and efficient.

No matter what you spend your workday doing--bank teller, clerk at the grocery store, truck driver, computer tech--you want to re-energize and refresh by relieving the stress that is building up in your body and mind.

If you sit all day, a good rejuvenation break is any kind of physical activity, such as getting fresh air outdoors for 10-15 minutes, listening to music as you move, taking a walk indoors, doing the stairs or walking in nature. If you are active all day, taking a break to destress your joints, muscles and mind is important.

Hydration

Hydration is critically important because your body is 70 percent water. Every cell, tissue, and organ in the body needs water to function. Water also regulates your body temperature, lubricates your joints, transports nutrients and energy to the body, increases immunity strength, produces digestive enzymes, and eliminates toxins. That is a lot. Most people live in some state of dehydration. It is important to drink 10-12 glasses of pure living water every day.

Alkalizing - Quality of Water

This is one of my top 3 healing principles and it is always included in my keynote presentations. All things in our life, even invisible things we are not aware of, produce acid in our bodies. Let me give you some examples.

Environmental stresses include: pollution from vehicle exhaust and factories, pesticides, herbicides, and even medications (both over the counter and prescribed). Additionally, there are antibiotics injected into the cows, calves, chickens, and pigs that we eat. All of these things can alter our body chemistry and produce acid in our body.

Sugary drinks and processed foods also create acid in our bodies. Packaged foods entice us with their marketing and packaging, but the reality is they should have a poison symbol with a big X on them. Let's not forget about emotional and mental stresses. Unfortunately, the health risks are invisible. It's like radiation; you don't know that you've been exposed to it until you experience problems.

The problem with acid is that it ages you prematurely. Let's say you are fifty. That doesn't mean that your cells are that of a 50-year-old; your cells might be that of a 70-year-old. Acid also causes inflammation and creates an environment where disease can thrive.

That is where alkalizing comes in. When you get rid of the acid, you create an environment for health, healing and strength in your body. The best way to do that is with alkalized, living water. Most water you drink is acidic. A simple way to create alkalizing water is to add lemon, lime, or apple cider vinegar along with a small pinch of pink Himalayan salt (if desired- careful for those with blood pressure issues). Please know that just because you drink water and fluids that does not mean your body is absorbing them.

Since most likely you are also dehydrated, this solution kills two birds with one stone. You alkalize your body and hydrate at the same time. There are alkalizing water systems available on the market for home and business use. Having one of these systems is one of the most valuable things you can do for yourself.

For a free checklist of foods to avoid and foods that help alkalize you, visit www.lifestylewellnesscentre.com and diabeteswellnesscentre.com.

NOW IS THE TIME

I encourage you to take 100 percent responsibility for your health, starting now. You only get to live life once, and if you destroy your body with stress, (even unknowingly as I did) you may not be able to recover.

I am grateful to be alive. Most people who went through what I did have died. They never made it out of the hospital. My experience was a wakeup call, showing me that I needed to change my life. While I am still a very active entrepreneur who works hard, I continue to learn the value of listening to my body. I write this having recently returned from a retreat that I lead. I not only rejuvenated my body, but my mind and soul as well.

One of the things that changed my life was my near-death experience. Because of this, I want to help you, your family and friends. Stress can be very subtle, even silent for a very long time. I want to help you become more aware of your body so you don't go through what I did, or any other unnecessary suffering. It is unacceptable to me to become a statistic to a disease like my grandmother did. Even though she followed every directive her medical team gave her, and she had the support of her family, that did not halt her disease from progressing. I do not want to become one of the hundreds of millions of people with diabetes and thyroid issues who simply live in fear and frustration, and wait for the complications to show up and steal their quality of life.

I do not want to become a victim of any health or immune system challenge and I do not want you to either. Being traditionally trained and going back to university, earning my doctorate in holistic medicine and acupuncture, and studying at the National Guild of Hypnotists, I learned so much about what is missing in our healing process.

I knew I had to do more, and so I took 100 percent responsibility to learn and apply all that I could in my own life, and in the lives of those who came to me for service, council, and healing. My goal is being as proactive and preventive as I can, and sharing that with you. Is it time for you to take 100% responsibility too?

My health challenges inspired me to move beyond what I knew. I learned how to not only overcome stress but how to help heal the body. Now I can help you with your health and healing. If you have been struggling with stress, and are predisposed to immune system challenges, prediabetes, or have diabetes, or if you even suspect that stress is starting to affect your life, then this is the time for you to take action and join my community at www.lifestylewellnesscentre.com and/or www.diabeteswellnesscentre.com. I want you to contact me.

My chapter is a small example of the ways to de-stress. I would love to help you and show you how to integrate the top 10 healing principles into your life, because they will impact your energy and enrich your quality of life. Are you ready?

To learn more and to sign up for your free Masterclass visit: www.lifestylewellnesscentre.com and www.diabeteswellnesscentre.com

LOOK FOR THESE RESOURCES ON HOW TO DESTRESS:

- The Holistic Approach to Achieving Wellness
- De-Stress Today with Cheryl's 7 Step Easy Strategies
  (From my best-selling book *Success Starts Today*, co-authored with Jack Canfield and other professionals)
- The Entrepreneurs Guide to Success Without the Stress
- 7 Day Kick-Start Diabetes Wellness Makeover Program
- Free Masterclass - The Holistic Approach to Diabetes Wellness - You do not want to miss my 6 Week Holistic Diabetes Mini Series or my 6 Month Diabetes Lifestyle Makeover Program

And so much more....

Let this be a Healing Day in Your Life
Dream Big, Live Bigger!

Cheryl Ivaniski, D.Ac., C.H., RDH
Your Lifestyle Wellness Strategist

Step Into Greatness

LES BROWN

You have greatness within you. You can do more than you could ever imagine. The problem most people have is that they set a goal and then ask "how can I do it? I don't have the necessary skills or education or experience".

I know what that's like. I wasted 14 years on asking myself how I could be a motivational speaker. My mind focused on the negative—on the things that were in my way, rather than on the things that were not.

It's not what you don't have but what you think you need that keeps you from getting what you want from life. But, when the dream is big enough, the obstacles don't matter. You'll get there if you stay the course. Nothing can stop you but death itself.

Think about that last statement for a minute. There's nothing on this earth that can stop you from achieving what it is that you want. So, get out of your way, and quit sabotaging your dreams. Do everything in your power to make them happen—because you cannot fail!

They say the best way to die is with your loved ones gathered around your bed. But what if you were dying and it was the ideas you never acted upon, the gifts you never used and the dreams you never pursued, that were circled around your bed? Answer that question right now. Write down your answers. If you die this very moment what ideas, what gifts, what dreams will die with you?

Then say: I refuse to die an unlived life! You beat out 40 million sperm to get here, and you'll never have to face such odds again. Walk through the field of life and leave a trail behind.

One day, one of my rich friends brought my mother a new pair of shoes for me. Now, even though we weren't well off, I didn't want them; they were a size nine and I was a size nine and a half. My mother didn't listen and told my sister to go get some Vaseline, which she rubbed all over my feet. Then my mother had me put those shoes on, minding that I didn't scrunch down the heel. She had my sister run some water in the bathtub, and I was told to get in and walk around in the water. I said that my feet hurt. She just ignored me and asked about my day at school, how everything went and did I get into any fights? I knew what she was up to, that she was trying to distract me, so I said I had only gotten into three fights. After a while mother asked me if my feet still hurt. I admitted that the pain had indeed lessened. She kept me walking in that tub until I had a brand new pair of comfortable, size nine and a half shoes.

You see, once the leather in the shoes got wet, they stretched! And what you need to do is stretch a little. I believe that most people don't set high goals and miss them, but rather, they set lower goals and hit them and then they stay there, stuck on the side of the highway of life. When you're pursuing your greatness, you don't know what your limitations are, and you need to act like you don't have any. If you shoot for the moon and miss, you'll still be in the stars.

You also need coaching (a mentor). Why? There are times you, too, will find yourself parked on the side of the highway of life with no gas in the vehicle. What you need then is someone to stop and offer to pick up some gas down the road a ways and bring it back to you. That person is your coach. Yes, they are there for advice, but their main job is to help you through the difficulties that life throws at all of us.

Another reason for having a coach is that you can't see the picture when you're in the frame. In other words, he or she can often see where you are with a clarity and focus that's unavailable to you. They're not going to leave you parked along the road of life, nor are they going to allow you to be stuck in the moment like a photo in a frame.

And let's say you just can't see you're way forward. You don't believe it's possible. Sometimes you just have to believe in someone's belief in you. This could be your coach, a loved one or even a staunch friend. You need to hear them say you can do it, time and again. Because, after all, faith comes from hearing and hearing and hearing.

Look at it this way. Most people fail because of possibility blindness. They can't see what lies before them. There are always possibilities. Because of this, your dream is possible. You may fail often. In fact, I want you to say this: I will fail my way to success. Here is why.

I had a TV show that failed. I felt I had to go back to public speaking. I had failed, so I parked my car for ten years. Then I saw Dr. Wayne Dyer was still on PBS and I decided to call them. They said they would love to work with me and asked where I had been. I wasn't as good as I had been ten years before, as I was out of practice, but I still had to get back in the game. I was determined to drive on empty.

Listen to recordings, go to seminars, challenge yourself, and you'll begin to step into your greatness, you'll begin to fill yourself with the energy you need to climb to ever greater heights. Most people never attend a seminar. They won't invest money in books or audio programs. You put yourself in the top 5 percent just by making a different choice than the average person. This is called contrary thinking. It's a concept taken from the financial industry. One considers choosing the exact opposite behaviour of the average person as a way to get better than average results. You don't have to make the contrarian choice, but if you don't have anything to lose by going that road, why not consider the option?

Make your move before you're ready. Walk by faith not by sight and make sure you're happy doing it. If you can't be happy, what else is there? Helen Keller said, "Life is short, eat the dessert first."

What is faith? Many of us think of God when we think of faith. A different viewpoint claims that faith is a firm belief in something for which there is no proof. I would rather think of faith as something that is believed especially with strong conviction. It is this last definition I am referring to when I say walk by faith not by sight. Be happy and go forth with strong conviction that you are destined for greatness.

An important step on your way to greatness is to take the time to detoxify. You've got to look at the people in your life. What are they doing for you? Are they setting a pace that you can follow? If not, whose pace have you adjusted to? If you're the smartest in your group, find a new group.

Are the people in your life pulling you down or lifting you up? You know what to do, right? Banish the negative and stay with the positive; it's that simple. Dr. Norman Vincent Peale once said (when I was in the audience), "You are special. You have greatness within you, and you can do more than you could ever possibly imagine."

He overrode the inner conversations in my mind and reached the heart of me. He set me on fire. This is yet another reason for seeking out the help of a coach or mentor or other new people in your life. They can do what Dr. Peale did for me. They can set your passion free.

How important is it to have the right kind of person/people on your side? There was a study done that determined it takes 16 people saying you can do something to overcome one person who says you can't do something. That's right, one negative, unsupportive person can wipe out the work of 16 other supportive people. The message can't be any clearer than that.

Let's face the cold, hard truth: most people stay in park along the highway of life. They never feel the passion, the love for their fellow man, or for the work they do. They are stuck in the proverbial rut. What's the reason? There are many reasons, but only one common factor: fear — fear of change, fear of failure, fear of success, fear they may not be good enough, fear of competition, even fear of rejection.

"Rejection is a myth," says Jack Canfield, co-author of The Chicken Soup for the Soul series. "It's not like you get a slap in the face each time you are rejected." Why not take every "no" you receive as a vitamin, and every time you take one know you are another step closer to success.

You will win if you don't quit. Even a broken clock is right twice a day.

Professional baseball players, on average, get on base just three times out of every ten times they face the opposing pitcher. Even superstars fail half of the time they appear at the plate.

Top commissioned salespeople face similar odds. They make may make one sale from every three people they see, but it will have taken them between 75 and 100 telephone calls to make the 15 appointments they need to close their five sales for the week. And these are statistics for the elite. Most salespeople never reach these kinds of numbers.

People don't spend their lives working for just one company anymore. This means you must build up a set of skills and experiences that are portable. This can be done a number of ways, but my favourite approaches follow.

You must be willing to do the things others won't do in order to have tomorrow the things that others don't have. Provide more service than you get paid for. Set some high standards for yourself.

Begin each day with your most difficult task. The rest of the day will seem more enjoyable and a whole lot easier.

Someone needs help with a problem? Be the solution to that problem.

Also, find those tasks that are being consistently ignored and do them. You'll be surprised by the results. An acquaintance of mine used this approach at a number of entry-level positions and each time he quickly ended up being offered a position in management.

You must increase your energy. Kick it up a notch. We are spirits having a physical existence; let your spirit shine. Quit frittering away your energy. Use it to move you closer to the achievement of your dreams. Refuse to spend it on non-productive activities.

What do people say about you when you leave a room? Are you willing to take responsibility—to walk your talk. There is a terrible epidemic sweeping our nation, and it is the refusal to take responsibility for one's actions. Consider that at some point in any situation there will have been a moment where you could have done something to change the outcome. To that end you are responsible for what happened. It's a hard thing to accept, but it's true.

Life's hard. It was hard when I was told I had cancer. I had sunken into despair, and was hiding away in my study when my son came in. My son asked me if I was going to die. What could I do? I told him I was going to fight, even though I was scared. I also told him that I needed some help. Not because I was weak but because I wanted to stay strong. Keep asking until you get help. Don't stop until you get it.

A setback is the setup for a comeback. A setback is simply a misstep on the long road of success. It means nothing in the larger scheme of things. And, surprisingly, it sets you up for your next win. It tends to focus you and your energy on your immediate goals, paving the way for your next sprint, for your comeback.

It's worth it. Your dreams are worth the sacrifices you'll have to make to achieve them. Find five reasons that will make your dreams worth it for you. Say to yourself, I refuse to live an unlived life.

If you are casual about your dreams, you'll end up a casualty. You must be passionate about your dreams, living and breathing them throughout your days. You've got to be hungry! People who are hungry refuse to take no for an answer. Make NO your vitamin. Be unstoppable. Be hungry.

Let me give you an example of what I mean by hungry …

I decided I wanted to become a disc jockey, so I went down to the local radio station and asked the manager, Mr. Milton "Butterball" Smith, if he had a job available for a disc jockey. He said he did not. The next day I went back, and Mr. Smith asked "Weren't you here yesterday?" I explained that I was just checking to see if anyone was sick or had died. He responded by telling me not to come back again. Day three, I went back again—with the same story. Mr. Smith told me to get out of there. I came back the fourth day and gave Mr. Smith my story one more time. He was so beside himself that he told me to get him a cup of coffee. I said, "Yes, sir!" That's how I became the errand boy.

While working as an errand boy at the station, I took every opportunity to hang out with the deejays and to observe them working. After I had taught myself how to run the control room, it was just a matter of biding my time.

Then one day an opportunity presented itself. One of the disc jockeys by the name of Rockin' Roger was drinking heavily while he was on the air. It was a Saturday afternoon. And there I was, the only one there.

I watched him through the control-room window. I walked back and forth in front of that window like a cat watching a mouse, saying "Drink, Rock, Drink!" I was young. I was ready. And I was hungry.

Pretty soon, the phone rang. It was the station manager. He said, "Les, this is Mr. Klein."

I said, "Yes, I know."

He said, "Rock can't finish his program."

I said, "Yes sir, I know."

He said, "Would you call one of the other disc jockeys to fill in?"

I said, "Yes sir, I sure will, sir."

And when he hung up, I said, "Now he must think I'm crazy." I called up my mama and my girlfriend, Cassandra, and I told them, "Ya'll go out on the front porch and turn up the radio, I'M ABOUT TO COME ON THE AIR!"

I waited 15 or 20 minutes and called the station manager back. I said, "Mr. Klein, I can't find NOBODY!"

He said, "Young boy, do you know how to work the controls?"

I said, "Yes, sir."

He said, "Go in there, but don't say anything. Hear me?"

I said, "Yes, sir."

I couldn't wait to get old Rock out of the way. I went in there, took my seat behind that turntable, flipped on the microphone and let 'er rip.

"Look out, this is me, LB., triple P. Les Brown your platter-playin' papa. There were none before me and there will be none after me, therefore that makes me the one and only. Young and single and love to mingle, certified, bona fide and indubitably qualified to bring you satisfaction and a whole lot of action. Look out baby, I'm your LOVE man."

I WAS HUNGRY!

During my adult life I've been a deejay, a radio station manager, a Democrat in the Ohio Legislature, a minister, a TV personality, an author and a public speaker, but I've always looked after what I valued most—my mother. What I want for her is one of my dreams, one of my goals.

My life has been a true testament to the power of positive thinking and the infinite human potential. I was born in an abandoned building on a floor in Liberty City, a low-income section of Miami, Florida, and adopted at six weeks of age by Mrs. Mamie Brown, a 38-year-old single woman, cafeteria cook and domestic worker. She had very little education or financial means, but a very big heart and the desire to care for myself and my twin brother. I call myself Mrs. Mamie Brown's Baby Boy and I say that all that I am and all that I ever hoped to be, I owe to my mother.

My determination and persistence in searching for ways to help my mother overcome poverty and developing my philosophy to do whatever it takes to achieve success led me to become a distinguished authority on harnessing human potential and success. That philosophy is best expressed by the following …

> "If you want a thing bad enough to go out and fight for it,
> to work day and night for it,
> to give up your time, your peace and your sleep for it…
> if all that you dream and scheme is about it,
> and life seems useless and worthless without it…
> if you gladly sweat for it and fret for it and plan for it
> and lose all your terror of the opposition for it…
> if you simply go after that thing you want
> with all of your capacity, strength and sagacity,
> faith, hope and confidence and stern pertinacity…
> if neither cold, poverty, famine, nor gout,
> sickness nor pain, of body and brain,
> can keep you away from the thing that you want…
> if dogged and grim you beseech and beset it,
> with the help of God, you will get it!"

Branding Small Business

RAYMOND AARON

Branding is an incredibly important tool for creating and building your business. Large companies have been benefiting from branding ever since people first started selling things to other people. Branding made those businesses big.

If you're a small business owner, you probably imagine that small companies are different and don't need branding as much as large companies do. Not true. The truth is small businesses need branding just as much, if not more, than large companies.

Perhaps you've thought about branding, but assumed you'd need millions of dollars to do it properly, or that branding is just the same thing as marketing. Nothing could be further from the truth.

Marketing is the engine of your company's success. Branding is the fuel in that engine.

In the old days, salespeople were a big part of the selling process. They recommended one product over another and laid out the reasons why it was better. Salespeople had credibility because they knew about all the products, and customers often took the advice they had to offer.

Today, consumers control the buying process. They shop in big box stores, super-sized supermarkets, and over the Internet — where there are no salespeople. Buyers now get online and gather information beforehand. They learn about all the products available and look to see if there really is any difference between them. Consumers also read reviews and check social media to see if both the company and the product are reputable. In other words, they want to know what the brand is all about.

The way of commerce used to be: "Nothing happens till something is sold." Today it's: "Nothing happens till something is branded!"

DEFINING A BRAND

A brand is a proper name that stands for something. It lives in the consumer's mind, has positive or negative characteristics, and invokes a feeling or an image. In short, it's a person's perception of a product or a company.

When all goes well, consumers associate the same characteristics with a brand that the company talks about in its advertising, public relations, marketing and sales materials. Of course, when a product doesn't live up to what the company says about it, the brand gets a bad reputation. On the other hand, if a product or service over-delivers on the promises made, the brand can become a superstar.

RECOGNIZING BRANDING AND ITS CHARACTERISTICS

Branding is the science and art of making something that isn't unique, unique. Branding in the marketplace is the same as branding on a ranch. On a ranch, ranchers use branding to differentiate their cattle from every other rancher's cattle (because all cattle look pretty much the same). In the marketplace, branding is what makes a product stand out in a crowd of similar products. The right branding gets you noticed, remembered and sold — or perhaps I should say bought, because today it is all about buying, not selling.

There are four main characteristics of branding that make it an integral part of the marketing and purchasing process.

1. Branding makes you trustworthy and known

Branding makes a product more special than other products. With branding, a normal, everyday product has a personality, and a first and last name, and people know who you are.

In today's marketplace, most products are, more or less, just like their competition. Toilet paper is toilet paper, milk is milk, and a grocery store by any other name is still a grocery store. However, branding takes a product and makes it unique. For example, high-quality drinking water is available from just about every tap in the Western world and it's free, but people pay good money for it when it comes in a bottle. Branding takes bottled water and makes Evian.

Furthermore, every aspect of your brand gives potential customers a feeling or comfort level that they associate with you. The more powerful and positive that feeling is, the more easily and more frequently they will want to do business with you and, indeed, will do business with you.

2. Branding differentiates you from others

Strong branding makes you better than your competition, and makes your product name memorable and easy to remember. Even if your product is absolutely the same as every other product like it, branding makes it special. Branding makes it the first product a consumer thinks about when deciding to make a purchase.

Branding also makes a product seem popular. Everyone knows about it, which implicitly says people like it. And, if people like it, it must be good.

3. Branding makes you worth more money

The stronger your branding is, the more likely people are willing to spend that little bit extra because they believe you, your product, your service, or your business are worth it. They may say they won't, but they will. They do it all the time.

For example, a one-pound box of Godiva chocolates costs about $40; the same weight of Hershey's Kisses costs about $4. The quality of the chocolate isn't ten times greater. The reason people buy Godiva is that the brand Godiva means "gift" whereas the brand Hershey means "snack". Gifts obviously cost more than snacks.

4. Branding pre-sells your product

In the buying age, people most often make the decision on which products to pick up before they walk into the store. The stronger the branding, the more likely people are to think in terms of your product rather than the product category. For example, people are as likely, maybe even more likely, to add Hellmann's to the shopping list as they are to write down simply mayo. The same is true for soda, ketchup, and many other products with successful, strong branding.

Plus, as soon as a shopper gets to the shelf, branding can provide a quick reminder of what products to grab in a few ways:

- An icon or logo
- A specific color
- An audio icon

BRANDING IN A SMALL BUSINESS

Big companies spend millions of dollars on advertising, marketing, and public relations (PR) to build recognition of a new product name. They get their selling messages out to the public using television, radio, magazines, and the Internet. They can even throw money at damage control when necessary. The strategies for branding are the same in a small business, but the scale, costs, and a few of the tactics change.

Make your brand name work harder

The name of a small business can mean everything in terms of branding. Your brand name needs to work harder for your business than you do. It's the first thing a prospective customer sees, and it is how they will remember you. A brand name has to be memorable when spoken, and focused in its meaning. If the name doesn't represent what consumers believe about a product and the company that makes it, then that brand will fail.

In building your product's reputation and image, less is often significantly more. Make sure the name you choose immediately gives a sense of what you do.

Large corporations have millions of dollars to take a meaningless brand name and make it stand for something. Small businesses don't, so use words that really mean something. Strive for something interesting and be right on point. You don't need to be boring.

Plumbers, for example, would do well setting themselves apart with names like "The On-Time Plumber" or "24/7 Plumbing". The same is true for electricians, IT providers, or even marketing consultants. Plenty of other types of business are so general in nature they just don't work hard enough in a business or product name.

Even the playing field: The Net

The Internet has leveled the playing field for small businesses like nothing else. You can use the Internet in several ways to market your brand:

Website: Developing and maintaining a website is easier than ever. Anyone can find your business regardless of its size.

Social Media: Facebook and Twitter can promote your brand in a cost-effective manner.

BUILDING YOUR BRAND WITH THE BRANDING LADDER

Even if you do everything perfectly the first time (and I don't know anyone who does), branding takes time. How much time isn't just up to you, but you can speed things along by understanding the different levels of branding, as well as the business and marketing strategies that can get you to the top.

Introducing the Branding Ladder

Moving through the levels of branding is like climbing a ladder to the top of the marketplace. The Branding Ladder has five distinct rungs and, unlike stairs, you can't take them two at a time. You have to take them in order, and some businesses spend more time on each rung than others.

You can also think of the Branding Ladder in terms of a scale from zero to ten. Everyone starts at zero. If you properly climb the ladder, you can end up at 12 out of 10. The Branding Ladder below shows a special rung at the top of the ladder that can take your business over the top. The following section explains the Branding Ladder and how your small business can move up it.

THE BRANDING LADDER	
Brand Advocacy	12/10
Brand Insistence	10/10
Brand Preference	3/10
Brand Awareness	1/10
Brand Absence	0/10

Rung 1: Living in the void

Your business, in fact every business, starts at the bottom rung, which is called brand absence, meaning you have no brand whatsoever except your own name. On a scale of one to ten, brand absence is, of course, zero. That's the worst place to live and obviously the most difficult entrepreneurially. The good news is that the only way is up.

Ninety-seven percent of businesses live on this rung of the Branding Ladder. They earn far less than they want to earn, far less than they should earn, and far less than they would earn if they did exactly the same work under a real brand.

Rung 2: Achieving awareness

Brand awareness is a good first step up the ladder to the second rung. Actually, it's really good, especially because 97 percent of businesses never get there. You want people to be aware of you. When person A speaks to person B and says, "Have you heard of "The 24/7 Plumber?" You want the answer to be "yes".

On that scale of one to ten, however, brand awareness is only a one. It's better than nothing, but not that much better. Although people know of your brand, being aware doesn't mean that they are interested in buying it. Coca Cola drinkers know about Pepsi, but they don't drink it.

Rung 3: Becoming the preferred brand

Getting to the third rung, brand preference, is definitely a real step up. This rung means that people prefer to use your product or service rather than that of your competition. They believe there is a real difference between you and others, and you're their first choice. This rung is a crucial branding stage for parity products, such as bottled water and breakfast cereals, not to mention plumbers, electricians, lawyers, and all the others. Brand preference is clearly better than brand awareness, but it's less than halfway up the ladder.

Car rental companies represent a perfect example of why brand preference may not be enough. When someone lands at an airport and needs to rent a car on the spot, he or she may go straight to the preferred rental counter. If that company has a car available, it's a sale. However, if all the cars for that company have been rented, the person will move to the next rental kiosk without much thought, because one rental car is just as good as another.

Exerting Brand Preference needs to be easy and convenient

If all you have is brand preference, your business is on shaky ground and you can lose business for the feeblest of reasons. Very few people go to a second or third supermarket just to find their favorite brand of bottled water. Similarly, a shopper may prefer one store over another but, if both stores sell the same products, he or she will often go to the closest store even if it is not the better liked one. The reason for staying nearby does not need to be a dramatic one — the shopper may simply be tired, on a tight schedule, or not in the mood to travel.

Rung 4: Making it you and only you

When your customers are so committed to your product or service that they won't accept a substitute, you have reached the fourth rung of the Branding Ladder. All companies strive to reach this place, called brand insistence.

Brand insistence means that someone's experience with a product in terms of performance, durability, customer service, and image has been sufficiently exceptional. As a result, the product has earned an incredible level of loyalty. If the product isn't available where the customer is, he or she will literally not buy something else. Rather, the person will look for the preferred product elsewhere. Can you imagine what a fabulous place this is for a company to be? Brand insistence is the best of the best, the perfect ten out of ten, the whole ball of wax.

Apple is a perfect example of brand insistence

Apple users don't just think, they know in their heads and hearts, that anything made by Apple is technologically-advanced, user-friendly, and just all-around superior. Committed to everything Apple, Mac users won't even entertain the thought that a PC may have positive attributes.

Apple people love everything about their Macs, iPads, iPhones, the Mac stores and all those apps. When the company introduces a new product, many of its brand-insistent fans actually wait in line overnight to be one of the first to have it. Steve Jobs is one of their idols.

Considering one big potential problem

Unfortunately, you can lose brand insistence much more quickly than you can achieve it. Brand-insistent customers have such high expectations that they can be disillusioned or disappointed by just one bad product experience. You also have to consistently reinforce the positives because insistence can fade over time. Even someone who has bought and re-bought a specific brand of car for the last 20 years can decide it's just time for a change. That's how fickle the world is.

At ten out of ten, brand insistence may seem like the top rung of the ladder, but it's not. One rung is actually better, and it involves getting your brand-insistent customers to keep polishing your brand for you.

Rung 5: Getting customers to do the work for you

Brand advocacy is the highest rung on the ladder. It's better than ten out of ten because you have customers who are so happy with your product that they want everyone to know about it and use it. Think of them as uber-fans. Not only do they recommend you to friends and family, they also practically shout your praises from the rooftops, interrupt conversations among strangers to give their opinion, and tell everyone they meet how fantastic you are. Most companies can only aspire to this level of customer satisfaction. Apple is one of the few large corporations in recent history that has brand advocates all over the world.

- Brand advocacy does the following five extraordinary things for your company. Brand advocacy:
- Provides a level of visibility that you couldn't pay for if you tried. Brand advocates are so enthusiastic they talk about you all the time, and reach people in ways general media and public relations can't. You get great visibility because they make sure people actually listen.
- Delivers free advertising and public relations. Companies love the extra super-positive messaging, all for free.
- Affords a level of credibility that literally can't be bought. Brand advocates are more than just walking testimonials. They are living proof that you are the best.
- Provides pre-sold prospective customers. Advocate recommendations carry so much weight that they are worth much more than plain referrals. They deliver customers ready and committed to purchasing your product or service.
- Increases profits exponentially. Brand advocates are money-making machines for your business because they increase sales and decrease marketing costs.

For these reasons, brand advocacy is 12 out of 10!!

BRANDING YOURSELF: HOW TO DO SO IN FOUR EASY WAYS

If you're interested in branding your product or company, you may not be sure where to begin. The good news: I'm here to help. You can brand in many ways, but here I pare it down to four ways to help you start:

Branding by association

This way involves hanging out with and being seen with people who are very much higher than you in your particular niche.

Branding by achievement

This way repurposes your previous achievements.

Branding by testimonial

This way makes use of the testimonials that you receive but have likely never used.

Branding by WOW

A WOW is the pleasantly unexpected, the equivalent of going the extra mile. The easiest and most certain way to WOW people is to tell them that you've written a book. To discover how you can write a book of own, go to www.BrandingSmallBusinessForDummies.com.

Sex, Love and Relationships

DR. JOHN GRAY

Just as great sex is important to lasting love, good health is important to sex and relationships. About 12 years ago, I cured myself of early stage Parkinson's disease. The doctors were amazed, but my wife was even more amazed. She noted that our relationship and sex life had become dramatically better. It turns out that the natural supplements I used to reverse Parkinson's can also make you more attentive and loving in your relationship. At that point, I realized that good relationship skills alone were not enough to sustain love and passion for a lifetime.

I shared many insights gained from my 40 years' experience as a marriage counselor and coach in *Men Are From Mars, Women Are From Venus*. And while my insights go a long way towards helping men and women understand and support each other, good communication skills alone are not always enough. For better relationships, we not only need to be healthy, but we must also experience optimum brain function.

If you are tired, depressed, anxious, not sleeping well, or in pain, then certainly romantic feelings will become a thing of the past. My recovery from Parkinson's revealed to me the profound connection between the quality of our health and our relationships. This insight has motivated me, over the past twelve years, to research the secrets of optimum health as a foundation for lasting love.

These are health secrets that are generally not explored in medical school. In medical school, doctors are indoctrinated into the culture of examining the symptoms, identifying the sickness, and prescribing a drug to treat that sickness. They learn very little about how to be healthy or to sustain successful relationships.

There are no university courses entitled "Better Nutrition For Better Sex". Drugs sometimes save lives, but they also have negative side effects that do little to preserve the passion in a relationship. Ideally, drugs should be used as a last resort and 90 % of our health plan should be drug free. From this perspective, the heath care crisis, as well as our high rate of divorce in America, is indirectly caused by our dependence on doctors and prescription drugs.

Most people have not even considered that taking prescribed drugs (even for the small stuff) can weaken their relationships, which in turn makes them more vulnerable to more disease. For example, if you are feeling depressed or anxious, a drug may numb your pain, but it does nothing to help you correct the cause of your problem. It can even prevent you from feeling your natural motivation to get the emotional support you need. In a variety of ways, our common health complaints are all expressions of two major conditions: our lack of education to identify and support unmet gender-specific emotional needs; and our lack of education to identify and support unmet gender-specific nutritional needs.

With an understanding of natural solutions that have been around for thousands of years, drugs are not needed to treat many common complaints. Some symptoms like low energy, weight gain, allergies, hormonal imbalance, mood swings, poor sleep, indigestion, lack of focus, ADD and ADHD, procrastination, low motivation, memory loss, decreased libido, PMS, vaginal dryness, muscle and joint pain, or the lack of passion in life and/or our relationships can be treated drug-free. By using drugs (even over-the-counter drugs) to treat these common complaints, our bodies and relationships are weakened, making us more vulnerable to bigger and more costly health challenges like cancer, diabetes, heart disease, auto-immune disease, dementia, and Alzheimer's. In simple terms, by handling the easy stuff (the common complaints) without doctors and drugs, we can protect ourselves from the big stuff (cancer, heart disease, dementia, etc.) We can be healthy and also enjoy lasting love and passion in our personal lives.

Even if you are taking anti-depressants or hormone replacement therapy, sometimes all it takes to stop treating the symptom is to directly handle the cause. With specific mineral orotates (something most people have never heard of) or omega three oil from the brains of salmon, your stress levels immediately drop and you begin to feel happy and in love again.

For every health challenge, we have explored the effects on our relationships, with as well as natural remedies that can sometimes produce immediate positive results. You can find these natural solutions to common health complaints for free at my website: www.MarsVenus.com.

What they don't teach in medical school is how to be healthy and happy without the use of drugs or hormone replacement. By refusing drugs and taking responsibility for your health, a wealth of new possibilities can become available to you. We are designed to be healthy and happy, and it is within our reach if we commit to increasing our knowledge.

New research regarding the brain differences in men and women reveals how specific nutritional supplements, combined with gender-specific relationship and self-nurturing skills, can stimulate the hormones of health, happiness and increased energy. Over the past 10 years in my healing center in California, I witnessed how natural solutions coupled with gender-specific relationship skills could solve our common health complaints without drugs. By addressing these common complaints without prescribed drugs, not only do we feel better, but our relationships have the potential to improve dramatically.

Ultimately the cause of all our common complaints is higher stress levels. Researchers around the world all agree that chronic stress levels in our bodies provide a basis for any and all disease to take hold. An easy and quick solution for lowering our stress reactions is specific nutritional support combined with gender-smart relationship skills. Extra nutritional support is needed because stress depletes the body very quickly of essential nutrients. When a car engine is running more quickly, it uses fuel more quickly. When we are stressed, we need both extra nutrients and extra emotional support. Understanding what we need to take and where to get it requires education. Every week day at www.MarsVenus.com I have a live daily show where I freely answer questions and provide this much-needed new gender-specific insight.

At www.MarsVenus.com, we are happy to share what we have learned for creating healthy bodies and positive relationships. You can find a host of natural solutions for common complaints and feel confident that you have the power to feel fully alive with an abundance of energy and positive feelings that will enrich all your relationships.

Never Give Up!

My Journey to Purpose

VIVIAN STARK

NEVER GIVE UP: GROWTH AND SUCCESS COME IN INCREMENTS, NOT LEAPS

My desire is to encourage you with my life story. I have spent my life learning and improving myself, and I am thrilled to share what I have learned with you. Today I am living my definition of success. I have said NO TO THE PITY PARTY! Personal growth and development are a daily diet staple, and have fueled me in my business and entrepreneurial successes.

I wake up every day, knowing I am living my life with purpose, knowing I am the kind of person I always wanted to be. I have faced many challenges; my story has failures as well as successes. But I have learned that setbacks are only a part of the story; they are not the whole story. The story keeps going as long as you keep trying. You can choose to quit and make the story end in failure or dissatisfaction, or you can choose to keep trying and make your story what you want it to be.

Never give up. Success and growth do not come in leaps, they come in increments. The challenges will keep coming at you and sometimes it feels like two steps forward, one step back. But remember you did have those steps forward and you will again – if you never give up. You can choose to be overcome by dreck that life throws at you, or you can open your eyes to the love and opportunity that are always there too. You can have the life you want if you never, never, never give up on what is important – You.

IT IS YOUR LIFE - LIVE IT YOUR WAY

My life is my own for the making, but I did not always know this. I lived a very sheltered life as a child, fiercely protected by my overbearing Greek parents. I was not allowed to do the 'normal' girl things, like have sleepovers or join the Girl Guides to be a Brownie. When I was older I was not allowed to date for fear of gossip within my community. My parents lived in fear of the unknown. I lived in fear of being reprimanded if I disobeyed.

Despite my fear, insecurity, and extremely introverted personality, I pushed myself to exert my independence and fulfill certain goals that I set out for myself. From a very young age, I felt that I always needed to prove myself. To prove that I was pretty enough, smart enough, or even good enough. I worked tirelessly to achieve my dreams, never sharing them with anyone for fear of being ridiculed.

I began pursuing my goals as a young teen who wanted to fit in. I lived in an affluent area of Vancouver and always felt out of place. I did not have all the cool clothes that everyone else had, so I worked with my brother as a gardener cutting grass for one of my dad's clients. I saved my money and bought the clothes I wanted so that I would 'fit in' with the crowd. Despite this, I never felt that I fit in with other kids.

I was a rather "ugly duckling" as a younger girl, with a massive overbite and awkward shyness about me. After having braces, I felt my "ugly" stage was behind me and I decided to take a modeling class over several weeks one summer when I was in high school. My parents did not support me in this decision, so I chose to pay for it myself. The modeling class cost $800. I worked at Zellers for $3.00/hour. I persevered and saved enough money to pay for the class.

It turns out that the modeling class was just what I needed. I learned how to carry myself and exude confidence. After finishing the class, I took several modeling jobs and had many successes in my short modeling career. I made the cover of the then prestigious Back to School catalog for Eaton's Department Store, along with several other fun and exciting modeling adventures.

My modeling highlight and a fond memory was when I was hired for a ski catalog. (They wanted a curvy model. Who knew that sometimes it pays to not be super skinny!) We were taken up to the top of Blackcomb Mountain by helicopter before the official ski season opening. I remember having to jump out of the helicopter into three feet of snow because the helipad was snow-covered, and the helicopter could not land. I was paid $850 per day for three days. It was a dream come true. I felt validated.

When I was nineteen I began dating a handsome Greek guy I met at a wedding. Before I knew it, his parents and my parents got together and began planning our wedding. I literally cannot remember him actually asking me to marry him. How sad is that? Some time before our wedding I found out that he was into drugs and was still seeing his ex-girlfriend. I broke up with him and cancelled the wedding.

To escape well-meaning friends and relatives, I took an extended holiday to Greece where I could recover from the breakup. Armed with my modeling composite cards and my lovely, fashionable clothes, I hoped to land some modeling jobs while I was there. Instead, I met another handsome Greek guy who was smooth and charming. He swept me off my feet.

In classic old-school Greek fashion, my mom flew to Greece to check him out and determine whether he was a suitable partner for me. Like I said, I lived a sheltered life. She approved and, after a civil wedding in Canada, I moved to Greece to start my life with my new husband.

The first thing he did when we settled in to our home was give away all my beloved clothes. He proceeded to tell me what I could and could not do, where I could and could not go, and how I had to act. He, like my parents, was consumed with what other people thought of him and now me. I was terrified. What had I done?

I realized very quickly I had made a huge mistake and wanted to leave him and go back to Canada. To my surprise, I was already pregnant. Too embarrassed to tell anyone my sad state of affairs, I stayed in Greece. I had made an agreement with my husband that our children would be born in Canada. I did not want to risk my children having to go to the army if they were boys. After my first son was born, I returned to Greece.

When I became pregnant with my second son, I decided to leave Greece, not to return. I told my husband I was going back to Canada and he could come with me or not. He chose to move to Canada with me, but we broke up after a few years. Our marriage was just not meant to be, but I was blessed with two healthy, adorable and rambunctious boys that I loved so much.

Once divorced, my husband went back to Greece to avoid paying child support and to be near his momma, so she could pamper and take care of him. (It's a Greek thing. He was a huge momma's boy. Never again.) I was determined that my two boys would never be momma's boys!

THE SETBACK IS NOT THE END OF THE STORY PUSH YOURSELF TO YOUR NEXT GREAT CHAPTER

For the next few years, I lived in low-income housing while raising my boys and working at Woodward's department store. Then, I left my job at Woodward's and began a career in banking. I started out on the front lines working as a teller. After six weeks I was promoted to the prestigious side counter position. Within a year I was promoted again to managing tens of millions of dollars of lawyers' trust funds in an exclusive, independent position.

I was always pushing myself to be better, to do more, be more, have more so I could give more. I wanted to improve myself and my income to support my family. I had an internal drive to never give up. I wanted to prove everyone wrong. I would make it. I could do this! During these years I learned to appreciate life's lessons and gifts and I continued to grow.

Ten years after my first marriage, I married a second time. I became pregnant soon after our wedding in Hawaii but spent most of my time during our marriage being neglected by my husband. As soon as my daughter was born, I no longer existed in his eyes. I later found out that my husband had a girlfriend before, during, and after our entire marriage. He worked with her; she was married, too, and the four of us occasionally hung out together as couples. Needless to say, the marriage did not last, but I would not change a thing as I have my beautiful daughter from that relationship.

I spent the next years relentlessly trying to find my passion. I worked in banking, direct sales, office supplies, a genealogical search company, and as a sales manager for a roofing distribution company. I also went to night school while working full-time and raising my kids, to get my diploma in International Trade. Additionally, I began a calling card company in Santiago, Chile that I launched at the Canada/Chile Trade Mission in 2003.

OPPORTUNITY KEEPS KNOCKING, SO OPEN THE DOOR!

I was very proud of the calling card company. It was a crazy dream, but I wanted to make it happen. Recognizing a huge opportunity, I wanted to offer an affordable service that we took for granted in Canada. The large telecommunications companies had a very different view on my entry to the marketplace and I was forced out of business when they pressured my distribution channel to drop me. Unfortunately, my venture was short-lived after significant effort and money had been invested. I planned to travel back to Chile to negotiate a deal with another distributor when I was rear-ended in a car accident and suffered severe whiplash, leaving me unable to travel. I had to move on from this company but by this time I knew it was not the end. I knew other opportunities would come my way.

By 2007, I was working for a computer company selling proprietary software and hardware for restaurants. My expertise in sales and customer service had grown significantly by then. I had come a long way from the introverted little Greek girl who thought she was not good enough. With perseverance, training, and a belief in myself I had become a great salesperson.

I loved working with customers and was enjoying my new career when I began having severe migraines regularly. I was also having issues with my sinuses. I thought I probably had a severe sinus infection, but my nose and upper gums were numb, which was troubling.

That August was one big headache, literally. I had eight migraines that month and each one put me down for two to five days. I went to the doctor and had several tests run, including a CT scan. After the CT scan doctors finally determined the cause of my sinus trouble and migraines.

I will never forget that day. The doctor's office called and scheduled me for a 7:00 PM appointment. The doctor came in and told me that I had a brain tumor and that she was very sorry, but she did not know whether it was benign or malignant. She had not consulted a neurologist before meeting with me. I drove home in a state of shock and called my mom to tell her the news.

I learned that I had a meningioma, a benign brain tumor. After an MRI, I learned it measured 3.3 x 3.4 x 4.4 cm, was in my right frontal lobe, and had probably been growing for twenty or thirty years. Only recently had it grown large enough to begin causing migraines, sinus pain, and facial numbness.

Within a month I would be having major brain surgery to remove the tumor. Oddly enough, I was not scared until the day of the surgery, when it really sunk in. I had been told that the tumor was in an excellent location for surgery and that I would not need chemo or radiation afterwards. The tumor was not going to kill me. But with any surgery there is always a risk.

I do not remember much that happened the first week or so post-surgery. When I really came around and began noticing things, the first thing that caught my attention was that I was having significant vision problems. The brain surgeon had touched a nerve in my right eye, causing fourth nerve palsy. I always had this weird talent to do crazy thing with my eyes and move them independently, but this was something I could not control. I had severe double vision. I could only see straight when I looked through a very narrow view if I tilted my chin down. And I could not look to my left at all. When I tried, I lost all focus and control of my eyes.

This condition is similar to a child having a wandering eye. Actually, I had to be seen at Vancouver Children's Hospital to have my condition monitored. This was a very challenging time for me. It was one of the worst times of my life. I had so much stress and anxiety wondering if my vision would be like this forever. My head was permanently disfigured, leaving my self-esteem at an all-time low. My jaw was so stiff from surgery that I could barely open my mouth to eat. I was house-bound, and unable to walk up or down stairs without assistance. I could not read or watch TV to occupy myself because I was constantly dizzy. Every negative thought you could possibly imagine ran through my mind thousands of times each day. I wish I had known then what I know now about keeping a positive mindset, the healing powers of affirmations, an attitude of gratitude, and the law of attraction.

I cannot stress enough how important it is to reach out to family and friends to help you during a medical crisis (or any crisis, for that matter). Having people who love you to support you is so important. Being the independent person that I am, I did not ask for much help. Silly me. Stupid me, actually. I did not want to worry my kids any more than they already were. My mother was such an angel. She lived nearby and prepared meals for us, but for the most part, I was alone in my thoughts in a very dark place.

About five weeks into my recovery, I met someone online. Bored out of my mind, I had gone on a dating site, half-blind, looking for strangers to converse with me. Talk about being desperate! For our first meeting, I rode the bus to downtown Vancouver where we met for a drink. He must have thought I was rather forward on a first date when I grabbed his arm to walk up a few stairs. Little did he know that I grabbed his arm so that I would not fall flat on my face.

We hit it off and developed a relationship. He picked me up every day for several weeks and took me out on his random errands just to get me out of the house. Sometimes we would just hang out. At first, I only told him that I'd had a recent eye surgery. Eventually I told him the extent of the surgery. He was also having some challenges in his life, so it was wonderful to be able to help each other. I cannot tell you what a godsend he was for me. He came into my life exactly when I needed him, and I am forever grateful for what he did for me.

Worried about losing my job, I returned to work twelve weeks post-surgery. I was worried about paying my bills and the mortgage on the house I had recently purchased. I needed the money, or so I thought. In hindsight, that was the worst decision I could have made. I suffered with migraines and vision issues for several weeks before the universe decided I'd had enough. All of the senior managers, including me, were laid off from our jobs. It was the biggest blessing.

I did not work for two years. It was a very trying time. The line of credit was on a steady increase as the months went by, but I needed to heal. My vision took over a year to somewhat normalize, and the severe numbness in my face post surgery lasted for several years.

During this period, I had a lot of time to think. My surgery was a life-changing experience. I could have died. I decided to take on a totally different view on life from this time forward. From this point on, any time an opportunity presented itself I was going to take it.

DEFINE YOUR WORK AND WHAT YOU NEED

Knowing that after all my health problems I would need a job that allowed me to make my health a priority, I decided to choose a job that would work for me rather than choosing to work for the job. I started slowly by taking a 100% sales commission, part-time position that allowed me to work as much or as little as I wanted.

I told my bosses about my medical condition, and that I was not sure how I would respond to being back to work. My boss told me that as long as I was meeting or exceeding my quotas that he would not micromanage me. I would be allowed to do my own thing, which was perfect for me. For some this would be a scary venture to undertake, but I was up for the challenge.

I pushed myself by working long hours, often answering customer emails at 6:00 AM before I went to work and again well into the evening. I needed to build up my customer base and wanted to ensure they were well taken care of. Within less than six months I was working full-time and making a full-time income. I was back!

After working for this company for about four years, a couple of millennials were hired into the mix, and that changed everything for me. I was working independently with little interaction with my bosses for the most part and the millennials were cc'ing him on every email they sent. This is when my interest in generational differences in the workplace was first piqued.

Although I enjoyed the work and my co-workers, my bosses were a different story. My work environment left much to be desired. Receiving year-end bonuses based on sales is a standard practice in the world of sales. When I did not receive a bonus at the end of 2013 because my boss said I was "already making too much money," I decided to look at other business opportunities. Forever the entrepreneur!

I continued working my sales job while seeking other opportunities. I joined an Australian direct sales company and quickly rose to the top of their company, becoming one of their top 20 earners out of 20,000 consultants. I had 1,700 consultants on my team and was the only director in North America. I earned free trips to Australia, Dubai, Aruba, Florence, Manchester, Dallas, and Los Angeles. I finally left my sales job in 2016 to pursue my new business venture full-time.

DREAM BIG AND HELP OTHERS DREAM TOO

I LOVED working with my team. Coaching and mentoring were my passion. In October 2016, I attended a One Day to Greatness seminar with Jack Canfield in Kamloops, BC. After a brief conversation with Jack, I decided to take his Train the Trainer course to become a certified Success Principles Trainer. The intention was to share this new knowledge with my team. I had found purpose and passion in supporting others to build successful teams. I felt fulfilled when I saw their self-esteem and confidence grow. They were conquering their fears and winning!

Unfortunately, I had to resign from the direct sales company in February 2017 when they started having issues with production and delivery. Later that year the company declared bankruptcy. I went through a lot of stress, anxiety, and loss of sleep. Panic attacks became the daily norm for me. I had known the CEO for over eighteen years and was completely in the dark about the state of the company. My team was upset and blaming me. I received a constant stream of Facebook messages and harassing emails. The downfall of the company was out of my control, so I had to bow out. But this was not my first time at the rodeo. I knew that my story did not stop here if I chose to keep trying.

I met someone in late 2016 who introduced me to an opportunity to speak and train businesses on generational differences in the workplace. I was fascinated by this as I saw the struggles my own millennial children were having at work. I look back now at the communication challenges that existed in my previous jobs and wish I knew then how the different generations think and process information. I wanted to more closely understand their environment and what I could do to help. It made perfect sense that bridging the generation gap would improve productivity, communication, collaboration, and make for a happier, more cohesive work environment.

I now know that the behaviors, attitudes, beliefs, experiences, and influences during an individual's formative years really shape who they are and how they behave in all areas of their lives. I was excited about my new-found knowledge, and planned to launch my speaking business by mid-2017.

I hired an image consultant to come to my home and do a complete wardrobe change to prepare me for my speaking career. Having someone go through my wardrobe and tell me to get rid of most of it was a very difficult experience. There were a few tears. I must have attachment issues! I eventually embraced the change and spent thousands of dollars on a new wardrobe to complete my new look.

Then, as luck would have it, I broke a veneer on my front tooth. No big deal, I thought. I had been through this before and would just have it replaced.

This was the beginning of my dental nightmare. From May 31, 2017 through December 21, 2017, I had twenty-six dental appointments to fix my front tooth. I began lisping and developed what doctors believe is a stress-related condition. I lost the saliva in my mouth, had burning in my throat from acid reflux brought on by stress, my voice was constantly hoarse, and I spent several months waking up with panic attacks. I never knew from one day to the next if I would have a voice or not, so I had to put everything on hold.

I saw every doctor and specialist I believed might be able to help me. I was taking six pills a day to help with my various symptoms. I hated this! I needed to feel better; I needed to heal my body naturally. I would not stop until I got the answers I needed. I moved away from traditional medicine, stopped taking all my medications, and began incorporating EFT (Emotional Freedom Technique), also known as Tapping, Reiki, and Bioenergy work, to heal my body.

Eventually, my body and voice were getting to the point where I could speak relatively well, I decided to move forward with the training business. I hired a business coach to get me on the right track, mentally and physically. He helped me tremendously during a very difficult time. I also attended Raymond Aaron's Speaker and Communication Workshop, which totally changed my training and speaking style. It gave me the confidence I was lacking and sent me on a whole new trajectory for my business. I began my own company, Gen-Connect Training in early 2018. It has been an amazing ride. I am much more at peace and ready for the next stage in my life.

LIVING IN THE POSITIVE HAS MADE MY LIFE

Although I have been blessed with many struggles, I have also enjoyed many successes. I have experienced relationships that did not work out, work and business challenges, worries when raising three children as a single parent, medical challenges, and many dreams and goals that seemed impossible. The one thing I always knew for sure was that if I gave up and wallowed in self-pity, I would be letting myself and my children down. That was not an option. Success was the only acceptable outcome.

I wanted to show my children what a strong, self-sufficient and resourceful mother I could be, and that they could always rely on me. I wanted to set an example and prove to myself and my children that I could provide for us no matter what. I am very proud of the amazing people my children have become; they are strong, independent, kind, respectful, and loving. This is the true meaning of success for me. Out of all the things I have accomplished thus far, they are my crowning glory.

FIVE STRATEGIES FOR A SUCCESSFUL LIFE

1) **Always have a positive mindset.** This is a crucial component. Before you get into the power of a positive mindset and the law of attraction, spend some time listening to what you are currently telling yourself. Check in with yourself. What is going on with you? We constantly speak to ourselves with an inner voice which is sometimes quietly whispering and sometimes yelling. Once you have spent a few days noticing how you speak to yourself, you may not like it very much; after all, you are your own worst critic. Be accountable for how you speak to yourself. Never fear, you have the power to change that inner voice!

Do you believe you are the product of everything that has happened to you in your life? Your inner voice may try to convince you that you are a victim of your circumstances and your past. Reflect and acknowledge the things that have happened to you and where you are now. Then prepare to move past them.

2) Shift your mindset using the law of attraction. You can influence things around you so that things happen FOR you rather than TO you. The universal principle of the law of attraction is that 'like attracts like.' The law of attraction manifests through your thoughts by drawing to you not only thoughts and ideas that are alike, but also people who think like you, along with corresponding situations and possibilities. It is the magnetic power of the universe which draws similar energies to each other.

The law of attraction is already working in your life, intentional or not. If you have a negative mindset, many unpleasant or unwanted things are probably happening in your life, and you may see negative things happening all around you. Think back to how you speak to yourself. Be mindful of your thoughts and that inner voice. Begin to think positively.

Along with thinking positively, begin to intentionally think and feel the things that you would like to have in your life. The most common things people desire are love, a career, good relationships, health, and wealth. Visualize a mental image of what you want to achieve. Repeat positive, affirming statements to create and bring into your life what you visualize or repeat in your mind. In other words, use the power of your thoughts and words.

Imagine that what you desire is already a part of your life. Acknowledge it with each of your five senses, to the extent that you can. Spend time imagining your life once you have acquired what it is that you want. Write out your affirmations and read them aloud at least once daily. You will begin to draw them to you when you act as though you already have what it is that you want. Persistence is key!

3) Take calculated risks. Do you encourage yourself to stay where you are and play it safe? Safe can be dangerous. I encourage you to take calculated risks. If you do not try new things you will never know how far you can go. When opportunities present themselves, jump on them. It may be your one and only chance. Push yourself and do not take no for an answer. Keep digging until you find the answer you want.

Quitting is always an option. Well, it is an option for those who are content living a mediocre life. Quitting is an option unless you want to live an amazing life with a purpose. If you want to live the life of your dreams, you must not give up. Do not give up and never stop learning. If you continue to learn, you will continue to grow both personally and professionally.

4) Appreciate all of life's lessons and gifts with an attitude of gratitude. Learn and grow from your failures. Let life's challenges teach you to persevere even when all you want to do is give up. Remind yourself that the only outcome you will accept is success.

5) NEVER Give Up. We all face adversities and challenges in life. It takes character, drive, and a positive mindset to persevere, overcome, and excel in life. The only person who can stop you from achieving your goals is you. If I can do it, so can you. Go for it!

Do you, your team, or organization want to be inspired to change your future and find your purpose?

Do you want to learn how mastering the Five Strategies for A Success Life can empower you in both your personal and professional career?

Do you want to say "NO TO THE PITY PARTY" and achieve the life you truly desire?

Vivian Stark is an inspirational speaker and corporate trainer living in Vancouver, B.C. Canada, whose captivating story will inspire you to live the life you want if you never, never, never give up on what's important – You.

As a generational and workplace effectiveness expert, Vivian's career centers around helping others work in a more collaborative and cohesive work environment. Her focus on engagement and accountability both in and outside of the workplace mirrors her personal belief of how you must take 100% responsibility in all areas of your life. Learn how giving up blaming, complaining and excuse making can lead you to live a life filled with peace, happiness and personal fulfillment.

To learn how you can incorporate her knowledge and expertise into your life and business with ease and confidence, reach out to Vivian at www.gen-connect.ca. Vivian is available for private or corporate speaking engagements.

Simple Steps for Big Results in Boosting Heart Health

RALSTON POWELL

"First say to yourself what you would be: and then do what you have to do."
— Epictetus

It strikes like lightning, and it steals loved ones from their families. It is the number one killer of men and women in Western societies; twelve million people die from it each year around the world. While some of its warning signs are obvious, it can come disguised as flu, headache, or just plain fatigue.

Some people have no symptoms and do not see it coming. They are oblivious to the damage that is already done until they are at severe risk of a catastrophe. It can happen at any time, even when they are at rest. If you do not act fast enough or seek help within minutes, it can be fatal.

What am I talking about here? What is this disease that takes lives by stealth, which can recur even when you've recovered from it?

A heart attack.

How many of you have lost a loved one, a friend, or a colleague to a heart attack? Sadly enough, there are many of us in these ranks. It is clear that people are getting sick and dying even at a young age. In fact, I first became concerned about the rising incidence of both heart disease and cancer when a member of my church died of Leukemia. This man was young, approximately 30 years old with a wife and young children. At the time, anyone who was diagnosed with cancer of the blood felt a sense of hopelessness. The second time I felt a sense of concern was when I heard of the death of a young man at a prominent company that I would visit daily. His diagnosis was a massive heart attack. Following that, a friend and co-worker who was having problems with his heart went on vacation to Guyana; in the heat, he suffered a massive heart attack and died. These experiences made me concerned enough to do research, and I found out that heart disease is stated to be North America's number one killer. People from all walks of life can be affected.

Heart disease is commonly reported among those who are physically unfit, carry too much weight, who smoke and drink heavily, and who are eating fat-rich foods. Yet it is no longer just the plight of middle-aged men. Women are just as susceptible, especially after menopause.

Tragically, there are now stories that heart disease is striking the seemingly healthy. You can be a marathon runner, observe a low-calorie diet, have manageable cholesterol, and you can still suffer a catastrophic heart attack without any notice or warning signs.

WHAT IS A HEART ATTACK?

Your heart is no bigger than a fist, but it is your strongest organ, and it works tirelessly from the time you take your first breath to your last. It is made of cardiac muscle, a specialized muscle that only exists in the heart, and, unlike muscles in our legs or arms, the cardiac muscle never tires.

The heart works to pump life-giving oxygen and nutrients in the blood to every part of your body. On average, it beats between 60-100 times per minute at rest. When you work out or are feeling anxious or angry, your heart beats more quickly.

Feeding the heart with blood are the coronary arteries. When there is too much cholesterol in the bloodstream, it gets deposited on the inner linings of these blood vessels, just like rust on the insides of old plumbing. These deposits, called plaque, build up and block oxygen from getting to the heart.

Decreased blood flow causes chest pain, angina, or shortness of breath. A complete blockage of blood flow can damage or destroy part of the heart muscle. Typical symptoms of an attack are anxiety, sweating, chest pain, stiffness or discomfort in the upper body, nausea, and stomach pain.

A person can survive a heart attack due, in part, to significant improvements in medical treatment, yet the statistics are ugly. More than 60% of people who suffer a heart attack die before getting the medical help that they need.

WHAT'S THE GOOD NEWS HERE?

The good news is that a heart attack is absolutely preventable. And its damage is reversible. If you've suffered the disease before, you can empower yourself to make sure you'll never be victim to another attack again. You can do so with minimal or zero drug use or surgical interventions, such as a coronary bypass or having stents placed in your arteries to improve blood flow.

You can lead a healthier life by making easy lifestyle changes. These adjustments are so simple you can see results within a month. Not only that, but you also reduce the risks against you by more than half.

Pretty good news, isn't it?

Changing the way you live is far more effective in prevention and repair than any number of drugs or tubes put into your body. Treating only the symptoms or the risks is taking the short-view, and that is why, once your doctor prescribes medication, you are on it for the rest of your life. You can stop playing the victim and take back control of your own life. By investing some time and committing to making the changes, you can protect yourself from this devastating disease and live life fully.

HEALTH IS OUR BIRTHRIGHT

It is time for a paradigm shift in the way we look at the prevention of heart disease and its therapy for rehabilitation. We must go beyond the conventional attitudes and treatments that limit how we can live healthier lives.

The first step we must take is to change the way we look at our health. I've always firmly believed that health is our birthright. Our bodies are wonderful, complex, finely-tuned instruments. There're no two ways of saying it - it is a miracle!

Picture this. You make a small cut on your finger when you're cutting vegetables. You may run tap water over the finger to stop the bleeding, pour hydrogen peroxide on it, and apply a band-aid. Since it was a small and superficial cut, you're completely healed within a few days. Voila!

But what has taken place without conscious intervention from you is a sequence of healing events. The moment the skin is cut, the blood vessels feeding blood to the area miraculously reduce blood flow to the injured area, like turning off the tap. Next, platelets rush to the scene. They have been alerted to the emergency by enzymes released from the damaged blood vessels. The platelets clot together to form a plug that becomes a scab to stop the blood vessel from bleeding further. In the meantime, signals are sent out to more platelets to come help at the site of the damage.

When the bleeding is under control, the constricted blood vessels open up again, this time bringing important white blood cells to destroy any germs or infections that may have gotten into the body through the wound. Then the body concentrates on healing and rebuilding. The skin on both sides of the cut stretches to meet in the middle, forming a scar, which may or may not disappear as the body adds more collagen to the area. The finger is almost as good as new.

Notice that I said all of this happened without any conscious thought on your part. That's because you are gifted with a terrific immune system with enormous healing power, which orchestrates events to repair and renew your body even as you're reading this sentence.

TIME TO GET SMART ABOUT HEART HEALTH

Why does disease happen then? When we are out of balance, both physically and emotionally, we suppress our immune functions. We turn our body from its natural alkaline state in which disease cannot flourish to an acidic state, which is ripe ground for illnesses like heart diseases and diabetes.

We need to look at health as being much more than just being free of disease. We should look at health as the perfect mind-body balance and the platform from which we can reach our highest potential, our greatest creativity, and lasting happiness.

At this point, I wish to reiterate that power lies within you.

What if there is a history of heart disease in your family? Doesn't it run in the genes? It is mistaken thinking to blame it on a shared heritage. Heart attacks are caused by how the environment affects your genes. So, really, it is what you eat, how much or little you exercise, how you handle stress, and environmental toxins that cause hypertension, high cholesterol, and other imbalances such as high blood sugar that increase the risk of a heart attack.

By turning from victim to someone who takes control with courage and determination, you will make healthy choices, add beneficial foods, exercises, therapies, and natural supplements to your lifestyle. Remember to be kind to yourself and take baby steps, but also congratulate yourself for every accomplishment, no matter how small.

CUT BACK RISK FACTORS

The number of things that make us more vulnerable to heart attacks are called risk factors. Research shows that poor lifestyle choices heighten some of these risk factors, including:

o Smoking

- o Unhealthy diet
- o Insufficient exercise
- o Chronic stress

These unfortunate lifestyle decisions lead to physical problems such as high blood pressure, high blood sugar, and a high level of blood fats. High blood pressure forces the heart to work harder than it should, causing it to weaken faster over time. High blood sugar speeds up the narrowing and the hardening of the arteries. We have already discussed the damage to the heart from high cholesterol levels.

Unrelieved stress from feeling anxious, lonely, isolated, or angry also causes significant damage. It is hard to accept that stress can be the single trigger for a heart attack. But stress creates that string of events that can lead to that one, catastrophic heart attack. Stress raises cholesterol levels, aggravates blood sugar imbalances, and elevates blood pressure, all of which make the blood more likely to clot.

In plain speak, the more risk factors there are in your life, the higher the risk you run of a heart attack.

SIMPLE STEPS, BIG RESULTS

There are steps you can take, starting now. It is better for you to add one simple change every day rather than attempt to do everything at once and give up down the road because you're overwhelmed by having to do too much at any one time.

Here are a few suggestions of what you can do:

1. Stop smoking. You reduce the odds of a heart attack from the very

moment you stop using tobacco.

2. Move it, move it, move it. Medical literature recommends exercising 30 minutes or more several days of the week. But in a pinch, even ten minutes of intense physical exercise goes a long way to making a difference. Take the stairs rather than the escalator, take a walk during lunch, get off at an earlier stop and walk the last few blocks to work or home.

3. Eat heart-healthy foods. Five servings of fruit and vegetables are a daily must, and if you must snack, pick vegetables like carrots, cucumbers, peppers, or fruit. Avoid the temptation to indulge in a sugar-rich pastry. Other heart-healthy foods are lean meats, fish, low-fat dairy, and beans.

4. Load up on antioxidants. These are the nutrients that repair daily damage to your arteries. Fruits and vegetables contain antioxidants. Green tea is another source of antioxidants; it has several powerful antioxidants that reduce cholesterol levels.

5. Cut back on fats. Reduce trans fats from margarine and avoid saturated fats, which are fats that turn solid at room temperature such as butter, cheese, and animal fats. Use olive oil as a substitute for butter or margarine and make sure you buy cold-pressed extra virgin oil as it has more of the healthy antioxidants.

6. Support with supplements. Pick antioxidant vitamin supplements such as Vitamin E and B vitamins, including B6 and folic acid. Add healthy omega-3 fats to your diet by sprinkling a couple of tablespoons of pre-ground flaxseed to your salad, smoothies, or cereal. Flaxseed oil, like fish oil, has been shown in studies to reduce certain cardiac risk factors.

7. Get regular check-ups. Consult with your doctor, but also broaden your choices by seeking advice from natural therapy providers such as

a naturopath or nutritionist. No one knows it all, and you must take responsibility for your own health. Conduct research and catch up on the latest reading.

8. Get good quality sleep. When we sleep, we give the body time and space to carry out the repair work to heal and to boost good health. Insufficient sleep is linked to weight gain, high blood pressure, and other heart disease risk factors. Sufficient sleep is defined as between seven to nine hours.

BOOST HEALING BY CREATING A HEALING ENVIRONMENT

Reducing stress is a major ingredient in the recipe for good health, so find ways to relieve stress in your life. Rethink a tendency to overwork in the office and sort out your priorities so you do not get too upset when work is frustrating. Build support groups and nurture strong relationships. Emotional support from friends and family are stress buffers.

Stack up on stress management tools. There are so many relaxation techniques available to any of us, such as yoga, Tai Chi, Qigong, acupuncture, or guided meditations. Yoga has become commonplace with many community centers offering classes. Acupuncture is recommended as a natural remedy to rebalance the body's energy flow, improve circulation, and blood flow to the heart.

Meditation has been shown to lower cholesterol and reverse any thickening of the carotid arteries. You can join meditation groups, download soothing music, and even find free guided meditations online which you can follow within the sanctuary of your own home. The idea is to have fun and experiment to see which one resonates best with you. Be committed and consistent with the relaxation techniques of your choice; you are making great strides towards better health.

Here's another tip: Do you know how health and beauty spas get you to slow down and chill out by playing slow, meditative music? Notice that they do not have loud rock-and-roll because meditative melodies slow the heart rate, while loud and fast beats rev up our natural heart rate. Prepare a playlist of soft, soothing music to help you take it down a notch.

PAY HEED TO THE MIND-BODY CONNECTION

Health is not just a state of the body, it is also a state of mind. Our bodies react to what we think and how we feel, and the mind-body connection is constantly in play.

It shouldn't surprise you that one of the best mind-body exercises is to have a good laugh. Laughter is the best medicine. We've all heard this before, and it is such a common saying that we often overlook how true the advice is. When you laugh out loud, you can't stay depressed, angry, or frustrated. In fact, a good belly laugh turns these negative emotions on their head.

When you're laughing until your sides hurt, you're doing many good things for your body: You're giving the T-cells a good boost. These are special white blood cells that are crucial to the immune system. They regulate the immune response or directly swoop down on infected cells. The T-cells need to be activated, and a good laugh will do precisely that.

Laughing promotes a sense of well-being. Endorphins are the feel-good chemicals that are produced from exercise. Laughter produces a healthy dose of endorphins and also contributes to an overall positive outlook on life. Those who have a more positive attitude tend to stay healthier or recover faster.

Your body relaxes for up to 45 minutes after laughing. Furthermore, laughter is contagious. Sharing a laugh with someone lowers barriers, promotes intimacy, and enhances relationships, all of which are good things that boost heart health.

Set your mind towards optimal health and successful healing. The change in attitude may seem like a small step, but before you know it, you've made giant strides towards maintaining a healthy heart.

Break Free From Your Pain Cycle

Winning the Battle and Conquering Autoimmune Disease

SEEMA GIRI

"It is not a journey of understanding; it is a journey of trust. It is a journey of surrendering every aspect of your soul over to the light."

— Panache Desai

Do you have an autoimmune disease? Did you suffer for years before obtaining a diagnosis? Have you been told there's no cure for your condition? If so, I suggest you look beyond your doctors and dive into the ocean of information that's available today regarding autoimmune conditions. You can also begin your journey back to health, take charge of your recovery by reading this chapter. That's right, I know you can reclaim your life. I've done it, and so can you!

> *"Sometimes it's controversy; but we all have choices that we make."*
> — **Solomon Burke**

There's a rising healthcare epidemic today. According to the American Autoimmune Related Diseases Association (AARDA), nearly 50 million Americans have some form of an autoimmune disorder. Business Wire, a Berkshire Hathaway company, has reported, "The global autoimmune diseases treatment market is estimated to grow at a [Compound Annual Growth Rate] CAGR of 3.80 for the forecasted period, and its market value is expected to reach $45.54 billion by 2022, up from $36.41 billion in 2016." Also, the National Institute of Health (NIH) claims that annual direct health care costs for autoimmune diseases are in the range of $100 billion (source: NIH presentation by Dr. Fauci, NIAID). According to the data published by the NIH, autoimmune disorders have been ranked in the top ten types of disorders leading to increasing mortality rates amongst women. These numbers are alarming!

As if this isn't enough, there's evidence today that the government, as well as agriculture and pharmaceutical companies, have been creating controversial dietary guidelines that primarily serve their needs rather than the needs of the people. This has been reported by major news channels, the Huffington Post and Marion Nestle, the consumer activist, nutritionist and academic who specializes in the politics of food and dietary choice. Roberto Ferdman of the Washington Post discusses this concern at length in his exposé "We Don't Know What to Eat." It gets worse. Soda companies are funding 96 health groups in the US—as covered by Time Magazine on Oct. 10, 2016. There's also evidence of an increasing number of illnesses nationally, globally and even in our children today.

So let me ask you, are we really getting objective information for our highest good? I certainly don't think so and it breaks my heart to see how little our lives are valued. What's the difference between lab rats and us? It's not as bad as it could be because there are an equal number of medical doctors, lobbyists, alternative medical practitioners and eastern holistic practitioners doing research and presenting their results. The recent movie "Heal" is a film by Kelly Noonan Gores about the power of the mind to heal the body, featuring Deepak Chopra, Bruce Lipton and Marianne Williamson. The film "Autoimmune Secrets" by Jonathan Otto also comes to mind. Then there's me taking responsibility to share my journey as a member of the global community.

> *"There are two primary choices in life: to accept conditions as they exist, or accept the responsibility for changing them."*
> — Denis Waitley

The good news is that you and your family don't have to be part of the statistics just mentioned. And you don't have to be affected by propaganda. You simply need to accept responsibility for changing your life and not accept anyone giving you limited information. This is more critical today than ever before.

It's important to make the CHOICE to take control of your health and that of your family. The answer isn't more medication. The answer is becoming more aware and educated. The answer lies in identifying the root cause. I'm passionate about educating you on this topic because life is a collection of precious, irreplaceable moments. Mothers should witness every moment of their children's lives. Children should not be robbed of their childhood. Fathers and husbands should not have to watch their family struggle and feel helpless. Families should not have to go thru the trauma of strained relationships because of lack of trust and differing beliefs. My family and I have lived through this. In Maya Angelou's words, "My mission in life is to not merely survive, but to thrive; and to do so with some passion, some compassion, some humor and some style"

> *"Our lives begin to end the day we become silent about things that matter."*
> — Martin Luther King Jr.

Will you join me in creating a revolution to break free from your pain cycle? I hope so. I'm going to share some of my story with you, and then outline the changes you'll need to make on your journey back to health, as well as some resources to help you.

"We are all Working Together; that's the Secret."
— Sam Walton

There's a quiet but pervasive problem in the world today. It's a sense of shame resulting from mental and physical health conditions. People feel they can't speak out, that others won't understand—and they're right! This is impacting families; it's impacting men, women and children (who are going to be the leaders of tomorrow). The problem can also be seen as a race to keep up with the acceptable norms of social and economic standards or as we say, "keeping up with the Jones'." Technology has helped increase anxiety with the ease of reach and exposure at the click of a button.

My focus in this chapter is going to be mainly on women in the middle class. Why women? Out of the 50 million Americans that have autoimmune disease 80 percent are women. I believe this is so because we are part of the sandwich generation; we need to take care of elderly parents and children. This leads to compromises in our own health. There just isn't enough time. And, of course, there are the effects of hormonal imbalances. Also, women are the primary caregivers in the family. They're at the centre of the family and have a great influence on everyone else. If we help the women—who are the counselors, the ones who spend the most time with our kids, and to who others constantly come to share their confidences— and they become whole people, what do think will happen to those around them? They're going to change.

Today, the majority of health issues are due to chronic stress, environmental toxicity and chemical toxicity. Our food is genetically modified and our soil is depleted of the essential nutrients. We aren't getting nutrient dense food. And don't forget emotional and mental toxicities. We don't realize the impact of these on our health. My own autoimmune story has primarily arisen from emotional toxicities and food, as you will see as I unfold my experience.

I'll even speak directly to the Indian community. Why? Because as a culture we keep our feelings to ourselves and internalize things quite a bit. The next epidemic is already here and it's psychological in nature. The stress women experience these days is phenomenal. This can be seen throughout society as a whole via school shootings and hate crimes. Resolving these issues requires getting back to basics. We need to slow down, breathe and listen to each other. We need to be authentic, open our hearts and share our issues. The more we reach out to our community, the easier it will be to support each other in coming up with solutions. Once this is done, you can have sustainable energy and health to be able to enjoy what you love to do as a professional or an entrepreneur.

Visit www.seemagiri.com for a free guide on: How to Reduce Stress.

With an autoimmune disease you tend to forget what normal is. There are layers of pain, layers of suppressed and unprocessed emotions—you know, the ones you say are ok but that still bother you in the back of your mind and that limit your life. To reclaim your health, you have to go through these layers, like you would an onion, and you have to reset and recharge at every step. Each layer brings a new insight and wisdom. While you may never return to the "normal" you used to know, you can absolutely create a new normal that is even better than before. This is like keeping your computer running efficiently; you have to begin deleting files that are no longer serving you and clean your hard drive. In the same way, from time to time you need to release your pent up feelings and resentments and allow forgiveness for others and yourself.

"Forgiveness doesn't excuse anyone's actions. Forgiveness stops actions from destroying your heart."
— Karen Salmansohn

You need to give yourself permission to let go of hurtful experiences and a painful past. This comes from acknowledging your situation rather than living in denial; taking responsibility and making the change. Master Choa Kok Sui, Founder of Modern Pranic Healing and Arhatic Yoga, states inner forgiveness deals with love and compassion, while outer forgiveness deals with the necessity to create order and justice. While you can forgive internally, the individual still must deal with consequences or punishment. For example, when a child steals for the first time, you can forgive them but still give age appropriate punishment so he or she doesn't steal again. These two types of forgiveness must be balanced, all while coming from a place of love for yourself and the other person. Otherwise the dis-ease manifests into disease.

"The journey of a thousand miles begins with one single step."
— Lao Tzu

I lived a life of confinement, isolation and depression for more than 20 years. I was misdiagnosed by multiple doctors for several years with anxiety, depression, stress, chronic fatigue syndrome, psychological issues and was even called a hypochondriac when the test results showed up normal each time. The worst part was that I had started to believe the pain, inflammation and lack of energy were all in my head. Even my family agreed with my doctors, saying that I needed to just get over it; I wasn't the only one in the world who had health issues, and I needed to learn to deal with it better and move on. Eventually, I was on over 26 medications, many of them causing additional side effects. Not a single bottle came with a warning that said, "may cause extreme sexiness" but rather, came with labels that said, "may cause dizziness, heart problems, depression, suicidal thoughts, etc." Many times I felt the side effects were more dangerous than my actual health problems.

The biggest problem with autoimmune disease is that you look perfectly healthy from the outside while you are having a tsunami on the inside that never ends. Life becomes limited to home and doctor visits, but people don't understand why. Secondly, it mimics many diseases that express themselves with lethargy, fatigue, dizziness, sleeplessness and inflammation. Doctors have to rule out numerous options. I was devastated and felt pushed into a corner. I was a burden on my family. The battle had taken so many years I could understand their frustration as caregivers. And even though there was a dim little voice in my head continuously saying there had to be a better way and that I was meant to have a better life, I fell into a deeper depression. I wasn't being heard by anyone and felt the best way to end everyone's misery was to end the problem, me. I had reached my breaking point and attempted suicide. That's how helpless and hopeless I felt. My thinking was that at least then my family could live a life without limits.

Following the suicide attempt, my family started to take me more seriously, particularly my husband, Upendra. I also realized that I did have a larger purpose in life, that I was meant to make a profound contribution to the world. Yet, there was still doubt in my heart. My greatest strengths were perseverance and courage. I had to use these attributes to fight for a life of possibilities and take charge of my recovery. I chose to listen to that tiny voice that said I was meant to have a better life and continued on my quest until I found a young doctor who believed me, took the time to actively listen to me, and finally did some new tests that enabled him to diagnose me with fibromyalgia and rheumatoid arthritis. Hypothyroidism was diagnosed earlier.

My journey to a "new normal" taught me many things. For example, I realized that the doctors were experimenting with different protocols. This knowledge prompted me to do my own experiments, even though my doctors had told me that lifestyle changes wouldn't make any difference to my condition. I had to try. I was encouraged to find that every time I made a decision, the universe always provided the right resources in terms of people and tools.

I first started making changes to my lifestyle with the help of my friend Mrs. Veena Singla, who introduced me to a whole food nutritional supplement, then exercise and personal development. I could tell I was progressing forward, but then I would go two steps backward, sometimes ten. However, I was persistent and consistent in my efforts to get well.

Because I had lost so much precious time, I hired several coaches to achieve my goals faster—the best investment I ever made in myself. Through their tested systems, life experiences and the perfect balance of empathy, ability to show me my blind spots, and not allowing me to hide, I got unbelievable results quickly. As I continued my journey, working with various therapists, counselors and coaches, I realized how many suppressed and unprocessed emotions I had bottled up inside. These were tough and scary to get through. It took several years of processing and removing layer after layer of emotion, but I managed to get closer to the core of the onion. There were some key pivotal moments that really impacted my life, but I kept peeling away those layers, one at a time.

> *"We didn't realize we were making memories, we just knew we were having fun."*
> — **Winnie The Pooh**

My problems began early in life. My parents were strict. They focused on excellence and were always setting new benchmarks (it was more like a sliding benchmark), that made me feel I could never reach their high standards and which led me to believe I wasn't good enough. My parents' constant pressure changed my basic nature, and I became a quiet introvert who kept to myself. You see, I was a naturally outgoing child who was unafraid of strangers (I loved to go on adventures and talk to all the people I would meet). But my behaviour scared my parents. Being in a country where language was a barrier and in a culture we didn't really understand, there were barriers my parents saw that I didn't see. To me, the locals were just people with a different skin color and language. My parents, however, felt I would be safer if I was quiet and controlled. I was disciplined constantly. I used to get a lot of punishments—from scolding to being grounded to taking away my partner in crime, my bike. This is when I discovered the bus. I started taking the bus to different parts of Berlin, the city in Germany where I lived. There would be times I would even come home at 10 or 11 p.m. I know, I know a seven-year-old should not come home so late, but it didn't phase me, as soon as my punishment was up I would do the same thing. I was hungry for adventures and expeditions! I could not stay in the box and have a life with limits.

Even in India, my playmates weren't limited to children but included monkeys, goats and cows. I was born in Shimla, India, a small town located in the middle ranges of the Himalayas. It's the capital city of Himachal Pradesh. Shimla is a lovely hill station that was the summer capital during the British ruling. I spent a considerable amount of time in the village with my grandparents where I had unlimited time to play. I've had a cow ram its horn into my stomach and pin me against the side of the house. I was bitten by a monkey. And I would hang the kids (baby goats) in the branches of our tree and leave them there (don't worry someone would get them down). This used to be all in a day's work. Now that I have children myself, I realize that I was a handful. My children really had a hard time in getting away with many things. My son, Aman, was equally as determined and managed to challenge me.

There are other significant traumas that have impacted my health, some from which I am still healing and find difficult to talk about. These unpleasant experiences led me to believe that due to the color of my skin and being a girl I wasn't good enough and should be invisible. At one point I was beaten so badly that I almost fainted and was covered in blood. I was also accused of stealing a pencil box, where the teacher pinned me against the wall and screamed in my face. These things happened in Owings Mills, MD, where I was the only Indian in the class. Then in Amherst, MA, when

I was ten years old, I endured the most traumatic experience in my life, one that would shape the rest of my future. It left me numb and speechless. I felt that the ground I was standing on was pulled from underneath me. I had nowhere to turn, no one to talk to, no one to believe me. I went thru life like a zombie. I wouldn't even feel the burn of scalding tea on my hand. I believed that I deserved bad things to happen to me.

I became secluded and was a total introvert, limiting my life to only school and home. I internalized a lot of my feelings. My parents couldn't really understand what I was going through. Sometimes I attempted to share my feelings, but I was told I was not supposed to feel that way and to study harder. My parents were working very hard to make a good living and provide a good life for us. They were also supporting my grandparents and my father's younger brother in India. My mother also started working retail on weekends. So that made me the babysitter for my two younger brothers. I didn't want to add to their stress.

About the time we moved to Germany I began the unexplainable manifesting of swollen hands and arms. Then a problem with my hip put me in the hospital for a month. They couldn't explain the issue. Again, we did the medical dance with the doctors: x-rays, tests, etc., with no logical explanations.

At first, I lived a double life. I had to be one way at home in front of my parents and another way at school to try to be accepted. At home I was quiet and invisible. At school I was more extroverted. But, eventually, I succumbed and lost connection to myself. I finally opened the box myself, stepped into it, sat down and closed the flaps. I lived life within the prescribed limit. If I liked the kind of things my father did, then life was easy. If it was anything outside of his wishes, it wasn't allowed. He had a certain idea of how he wanted life, family and kids to be. It was our job to fit in.

Over the years my health continued to be problematic, and I would see a series of doctors. They would do the same tests that would produce normal results. By the time I was in my 20's and married, I was sleeping 16 to 17 hours per day, and when I did get up, I felt like I had been hit by a transport truck. I was going from doctor to doctor to doctor, and it got to the point where I couldn't do the one-hour commute to and from work. I would fall asleep anywhere, even while driving. Now I was really beginning to think that I wasn't human. How can one have so many health issues/incidents without any explanations? I went wild in my imagination with the possibilities. The doctors were able to identify hypothyroidism fairly quickly. When I found out that there really was something tangibly wrong with me, I broke down in the doctor's office and cried. Six months later I was back in the same office because I was still having inflammation and pain. By now I was seeing Dr. Rusk at University of Pennsylvania. He was the first doctor who believed me, and who said my pain was real (that was another hug the doctor, crying moment) and sent me to an endocrinologist who confirmed, after a series of new tests, that I had fibromyalgia and the onset of rheumatoid arthritis. That was another joyous moment in my life. My pain finally had a name. Wow! Now I can be cured! I thought. Then came the shock. They told me there is no cure, just medications to help me manage the symptoms, and that as I age I may even become disabled. I felt like I was standing in court with a judge giving me a sentence: "You are hereby sentenced to a life of pain, misery and heartache. You'll be on medication for the rest of your life. You'll forever be dependent on others as well as a burden. Your life without limits has come to an end!" They told me to exercise—which was a catch 22. I was often in so much pain that it was impossible to exercise, and when I did exercise, I hurt more.

One day my doctor suggested that if I was considering pregnancy, I might find some relief there, as statistics showed that people like me often had permanent change after pregnancy. I wasn't considering pregnancy, but during this time we had a close family friend who had these two adorable kids, Mohit and Arjun. They were loving and authentic. The giving and receiving of unconditional love was amazing. The children were with me so much that people began to think they were mine, which finally got me considering to have my own. When I decided to go ahead, pregnancy was wonderful. I had no pain, my inflammation went away and I lost weight. I had never been happier and I even felt beautiful, something I had never experienced before.

Childbirth was tough though. I ended up having 40 hours of labour. I had preeclampsia, so they had to induce me. I eventually went through an emergency C-Section. However, for the first month everything was great. I couldn't believe I could love anyone so much as I did my son Aman. Then, I started to have symptoms of inflammation and pain to the point that I was bedridden for several months. I was so inflamed I couldn't even hold my baby. I couldn't do anything. There were times when my husband would just put him on the bed beside me so I could feel him and look at him. I couldn't do anything more than that. I finally said this is ridiculous; this is not the way I want to live. I decided I needed to be free from this torment. That was the beginning of my recovery.

So, here is what I learned… When you have a decision to make, always decide without worrying about the how. This is where courage comes into play. You see, in speaking to numerous people in chronic pain I've found they're so used to having a predictable life with support that they begin to enjoy the constant sympathy and attention they receive. As a result, they don't want to change; they're afraid they won't get the same type of love and attention once they are better. I had the same kind of feelings as all the others, but I took the chance anyway. I knew the life of appreciation and courage was far better than sympathy. I've never regretted it. And, now, I'm being recognized for taking action.

At first, it was just Upendra and I. We had family, but they lived far away. My mother had come for two weeks right after I had my baby, but that was it. Upendra was also quite amazing. He was my rock. He would prepare meals for my son and me before going to work, putting the food by my side within reach. I would have to start getting up 45 minutes prior to Aman's feeding. Yes, it would take me 45 minutes of pain, agony and tears to sit up to feed him. I had limited mobility. Upendra would come home and get back to cooking and cleaning. He wouldn't get much time to rest but he never complained or got upset. He was always very optimistic and looked ahead to the future. I guess it was easier for him than for me since he's a visionary guy. Which is why I didn't understand when he started to agree with the doctors that maybe the pain was in my head. Now that I think about it, we had an arranged marriage and had only been married for two years, so he didn't get the chance to know who I really was. We were a work in progress. With all my tests coming back as normal, I guess I would feel that way too. At that time though, I was furious that this thought could even come into his mind.

> *"The greatest gift of life is friendship, and I have received it."*
> — Hubert H. Humphrey

It was at this time that a close family friend, Mrs. Veena Singla, came on the scene. She was someone who really cared for me regardless of how busy she was with her own family. She also had experience with whole food nutrition. While growing up in India, her family grew their own food, so she had experienced the benefits of farm-to-table concepts, such as fresh fruits and vegetables. She was familiar with the Standard American Diet (SAD) and was also a cancer detection specialist, so she understood the science. In her research for better alternative supplements she'd come across a whole food supplement called Juice Plus. She ordered me to start taking it. I did so because I trusted her, and she was taking it too. However, it was the catalyst the nutritional base, for me to start taking responsibility for my own health. It helped reduce the inflammation and the pain. I was also able to get up and—within four months—start taking care of myself and my baby. This enabled me to make healthier choices. I ate less processed food, did a lot of research and went to a lot of seminars. This opened me up to a whole new community that believed in alternative methods and brought me into contact with people who had similar experiences, confirming to me that it was not all in my head, and that I wasn't crazy. I can't tell you what a relief this was to me. This is when I started to trust myself again. I started to believe that I could live a life without limits. I began to eat less meat and got off wheat, dairy, sugar and processed foods. I was able to exercise on a regular basis, and started working on my mindset.

> *"When I break the pattern, I break ground. I rebuild when I break down. I wake up more awake than I've been before."*
> — **Pluto**

The internal light and the constant voice declaring, "there has to be something better for me" and, "I am meant for so much more" was strong enough that I was able to break the pattern of my behaviour. Today I feel that my son, Aman, was the angel who came to me to make me take the steps I did. You see, doing anything for myself was very difficult. Indian culture is such that the focus is more outward. You are to be giving and caring for members of the family, rather than for yourself. I followed what my mom and grandmother did. I felt caring for my needs was being selfish. I think many women around the globe have felt the same way. Had it not been for the needs of my son, who was born in January of 1998, I wouldn't have taken that first step. I am in gratitude to God and my son for this.

I continued on with my healing journey and found women circles that supported my quest. I noticed a pattern that no matter where I went I always had one or two authentic friends who were there to support me. Whether it was to talk, help with the kids or embark on a girl's night out.

The integration of all of The Four Pillars of Health (nutrition, exercise, mindset and spirituality) has helped me be pain free. On April 27, 2000 when I held my daughter Ashima (my second angel) in my arms for the first time, I wanted her to not be burdened with the generational limitations and beliefs that I had. In order for that to happen I had to change and live differently. This meant overcoming the fears and beliefs I'd carried for several years. It meant breaking the pattern. Ashima inspired me to go even deeper. I wanted our background, culture and challenges to empower my children, to be their strength and foundation. I wanted them to be proud of their 5,000-year heritage. Aman and Ashima have also been great teachers to me. They taught me what unconditional love is. They showed me that they will love me for who I am, even if I don't do anything for them. As I've mentioned, I was taught by my parents that if I didn't do certain things, like getting good grades, then other things would be taken away from me. I was doing the same to my children, I would measure their love by how well they listened to me, but I think they must be old souls because they let me know it didn't have to be that way. You don't have to have one or the other; it's not "or" but "and." Imagine! Loving me just for me! That day I could feel years of built-up walls of shame and heaviness that I had carried all that time melt away. It felt like I lost 30 pounds that day.

It took a long time, but I finally realized all you have to do is begin to care for yourself. You need to show others how to love you by providing them an example through self-love. So often, you do everything for your loved ones, in the hope they'll return the same. But if you don't care for yourself first they'll have no idea as to what you really need in return. Could it be this easy?

By this time, I was hooked on Oprah's "SuperSoul Sunday." I had read several spiritual books by Ekart Tolle, Brene Brown, Elizabeth Lesser and learned how to live a conscious life where you make deliberate choices based on your values and your truth. In doing so, I finally learned that you must be courageous enough to take the first step towards change. As you do this you increase your energetic vibration level and attract like things. As you live better, your vibration increases and you attract similar things within the same vibration level. This is where the saying comes in, "change your thoughts, change your life." For example, those who always think negatively have negative things continue to happen to them. Similarly, those who always think positive, or are optimistic, have more positive things happen to them.

It was with these realizations that I noticed I was attracting more positive, accomplished and heart-centered women who took better care of themselves and their families and were pursuing their passions. I also noticed that I began to release people—even family members—who didn't support me, who were full of negative energy and who drained me of life. I learned that in order to change your life you must be prepared to change the five people you keep company with regularly. You'll find it makes a dramatic difference.

"When people walk away from you, let them go. Your destiny is never tied to anyone who leaves you, and it doesn't mean they are bad people. It just means that their part in your story is over."
— Tony McCollum

I started to believe in myself, that I was worthy, and I deserve the best.

"A woman who is convinced that she deserves to accept only the best challenges herself to give the best. Then she is living phenomenally."
— Maya Angelou

In 2003 we had the opportunity to go to India. We thought we would go for six months to see if the kids and I would be able to adjust to it. I was excited. I'd always wanted to live in India as an adult, and it was a great time for our kids to get to know our family and culture. Upendra has a big family: six brothers, their spouses, their kids and his extended family. This was scary because I didn't have any close friends or family there. This was an opportunity for us to not only serve our country and the people but also to reconnect with ourselves. Project management was our vehicle to do so. We built our company to 250 employees and trained nearly 100,000 people on project, program and portfolio management. While managing the operation, I trained and counseled professionals on which project management certification would be right for them, based on their years of experience and ambition. I started seeing a pattern of health challenges they were experiencing due to project deadlines and the odd hours required to support global operations. Many had shared that the reason for being in a company or a particular job wasn't because of their passion but because of need. I saw this as a global issue, not just in India. I believe a seed was planted, and I would often think about how I could contribute to people by helping them become healthier and living more fulfilling lives.

As I got to know my in-laws better, I developed a special relationship with my mother-in-law and one particular sister-in-law. Despite the vast differences of our upbringing, my mother-in-law and I connected deeply. She loved me like a son, calling me her seventh son. This is the highest honor she could give me. My sister-in-law's name is Nischal Di. How close are we? Even our birthdays are just a day apart! Nischal Di showed me the parts of myself I'd forgotten. On a regular basis, she would point out my strengths. In all these years, she was the first person who focused on that. She even stood up to my mother when she was not appreciating my successes as I wanted her too. No one had ever done this before. This is when I really started believing in Nischal. Who would take the risk to stand up to a parent if what they were saying wasn't true? In a country where I didn't know anyone, I found a deep authentic connection to someone who believed in me. As a result, the belief that I was meant to contribute in a bigger way was renewed in my heart.

My in-laws had always been progressive and open minded. They made it so easy and comfortable to adapt within the family and in India. The support was amazing and my kids learned the true meaning of a joint family. As a result, we spent ten years in India. It was incredible!

Unfortunately, at the peak of our business, my husband was travelling quite a bit which made it difficult to spend quality time together and the stress of the entrepreneurial roller coaster was so much that old and new symptoms appeared. I had to go back on some medications. During the same time in 2012, my mom was diagnosed with lung cancer. I thought that if my mom, who was so particular about health and diet, could get lung cancer, then anything could be possible with anyone. I was flying back and forth from India to the U.S. for nine months, before moving back to Maryland for the following nine months until she passed away. I was at the peak of my stress—with the uncertainty of my mother's health, the guilt of neglecting my kids and the absence of my husband. It also broke my heart to see my mother suffer. My doctor said I was a prime candidate for a heart attack or a stroke. When my mom died in May 2014, I relocated to Dublin, CA to focus on my health and the children. Over the next two years I was able to rebuild my health.

I've been in business with my husband for over 16 years helping him achieve his dream, and I never really had a connection to myself. I had become an introvert at my parents' hands, and I had followed their plan for me. Then I had been a mother and a businesswoman supporting my husband and his dream. I loved the entrepreneurial journey with my husband. I was able to support him in the way he needed, and I was shaped into a stronger, independent, sharper person thanks to Upendra's habit of throwing me into complex situations and making me fend for myself. Upendra was the blacksmith and I was the iron in the fire getting shaped. I am so thankful to him for that. But I don't think I ever knew myself. So, this is where spirituality really began to work in my life.

> *"Behind every successful woman is a tribe of other successful women who have her back."*
> — **Anonymous**

As I was exploring who I was through the journey of meeting phenomenal women in my community, I attended various seminars and meet-ups. I met a wonderful friend, Becky Diehl, who runs a forgiveness ministry with her husband Steve. Becky and Steve have been instrumental in helping me understand what forgiveness means. Although their program is bible based, I was still able to understand. Becky explained the message of God in a simple, practical manner that applied to today's life. This deepened my spiritual insights. She helped me reconnect with Hinduism and I truly began to understand the concept of God within myself. In fact, I can say through Jesus I was able to understand and connect to Hinduism better. This is a true integration of community and culture. I also began to listen to transformational leaders and coaches like Tony Robbins, Jim Rohn and The Secret team. One day when I was listening to Lisa Nichols, I learned why I needed to share my story. She said when you go through a major life challenge or solve a complex problem, the story is not yours to keep. You must share. You don't have to be a victim. You can change the meaning to be something that helps others—by telling your story.

> *"Always look at the solution, not the problem. Learn to focus on what will give results."*
> — **Anonymous**

The question in your mind right now must be what is the real solution? I believe this is going to be an ongoing exploration. Here are some suggestions to get you started. You'll need to keep in mind that everyone is unique and has specific needs. The key is to pay attention to what works for you. How well you do will depend on your commitment to practice.

- Look at holistic integrated healing. Our body is an integrated machine, and what happens in one area affects another. Holistic inquiry is to establish the root cause instead of just treating the symptoms. Sure, the medical community is crucial in our healing journey. But, we need to work as partners and be proactive rather than reactive. Functional medicine seems to address this philosophy. Find a doctor who shares your values and health philosophy. Ask lots of questions of your medical care team, and don't be afraid to get multiple opinions.

- Try an elimination diet. Start with eliminating gluten, dairy and red meat.

- Follow a clean diet. Add as many raw vegetables as you can. Eat organic as much as you can. You can even become an urban gardener, like me, and grow your vegetables on your balcony.

- Make sure your plumbing is working properly. It is important that you are expelling waste properly and regularly, both urinating and excreting. This is especially important before you detox. This happens when your gut is clean. Not passing waste is like not cleaning your fish bowl for months. Yes, it's really bad.

- Exercise consistently. What is the best form of exercise? The one you will do. The idea is to move your body. So do your favorite activity.

- Allocate sufficient time for sleep. This is when your body restores and recharges.

- Have the courage to listen to your inner compass and follow its guidance. Trust your gut and listen to your heart.

- Practice Daily Self-care and Self-love. This includes giving yourself permission to breakdown and cry

- Release emotions that no longer serve you. Open up space for new experiences to enter.

- Process unprocessed emotions. Let go and forgive.

- Ask for help. You're still a strong, respectable person, even if you ask for help.

- Stand up for yourself and make your voice be heard. This doesn't mean you have to be aggressive or put anyone else down. It does mean paying attention to your likes and dislikes.

- Reduce your stress. It's important to understand what triggers your stress and your flare-ups. When you know them, then you can actively remove them or avoid them. For a free assessment on How to Identify Your Trigger Points write to me at seema@seemagiri.com.

- Be in action!

It sounds like a lot of work doesn't it? To be honest it is, but it's so worth it! Right now you may not even believe that you can do this. It may feel overwhelming. I get it. I felt that way too. But the reality is that if you don't try, you'll never be able to do it. In fact, the very reason you should be doing this is because you don't believe in yourself enough to be convinced it will work. When you engage, you'll greatly change your confidence. The areas you resist the most are the greatest growth areas. Everyday that goes by where you don't engage in taking action towards improving your health, you're letting one more day pass you by that could have been more awesome. You might not care now, but consider this: as you lay on your deathbed and you review your life, the only things you'll regret aren't the shots you took and missed but the shots you never took that could have made your time on earth more magnificent. Not to mention that your family depends on you to make the changes that both you and they need. What legacy do you want to leave behind?

As Theodore Roosevelt says, "Do what you can from where you are with what you have!" This is actually a spiritual practice. Like Nike's slogan, "Just do it!" done consistently.

Life is not supposed to be difficult. You can get through it with ease and grace. The challenges we encounter are really there to teach us a lesson or sharpen us even more. If you stay true to your nature, life is easier and things start to fall into place effortlessly. The best analogy is that we are diamonds in the rough. The challenges are supposed to polish us so we can shine with our light; with the gift we're supposed to bring into this world. I truly believe that all of us have a unique purpose in life that is meant to be shared.

> *"The best way to get rid of the pain is to feel the pain. And when you feel the pain and go beyond it, you'll see there's a very intense love that is wanting to awaken itself."*
> — **Deepak Chopra**

Believe it or not, I consider my autoimmune disease a blessing in disguise. It forced me to reclaim my nature and voice in this lifetime, while I can still make a difference in the world. Today I'm a successful businesswoman, involved mother, supportive wife and active community member. I serve as a board member and I perform leadership roles in non-profits in my community. It gave me the opportunity to connect the dots and let me reconnect to myself in a profound way. It has also enabled me to connect more deeply and authentically with my children, husband and friends. I have thriving relationships. I'm pain free and off of 25 medications. I am down to only one and even for that, the dosage is reduced. I'm still making dietary changes. From time to time I get off my healthy track and indulge in sinful pleasures such as chocolate and ice cream. I simply get back on track without beating myself up and without judgement. I'm still learning. I'm a work in progress. Most importantly, I've found my purpose and passion. My life's work is to help women with autoimmune disease or symptoms, through …

- Personal, loving coaching to build your confidence and courage, and walk beside you through your recovery journey.

- Bridging the gap between your doctor's allopathic care and mind-body-spirit practices to create a holistic recovery plan.

- Advocating for you with your doctors and caregivers; work with your family to support you in your journey to a new life.

"The moment a woman decides to be unafraid she is transformed. When she recognizes the power and possibilities of her own strength and surrenders every fear to that power, she becomes the greatest version of herself."
— Diane Von Furstenberg

What can I do for you? As Denis Waitley says, "Time and Health are the two most precious assets that we don't recognize and appreciate until they have been depleted." The thing that bothered me the most was the time I lost being controlled by and managing my pain; time lost with family, time lost with my son and time lost where I didn't make a financial contribution to the family. While I can't recover that time, it has taught me to be more present and cherish every moment. This is my invitation to you to get your health and your time back, to design a life that brings you more control, energy, and balance. My work addresses the whole you—body-mind-spirit—and is drawn from the best practices in holistic healing, ancient eastern modalities, my own "kitchen-tested" practices and love. I want to hold your hand while you embark on your own journey of self-discovery—in the way only someone who has walked the path can. I've developed a program called "Take Charge of Your Health Blueprint for Women with Autoimmune Disease," which includes the strategies and life hacks I've created over the years. In this program you'll learn how to nourish your body and soul, how to energize yourself and how to take massive action and measure yourself based on your beliefs and standards. The point is to create simple systems that will help create a structure in your life that's specific to your needs.

My questions to you: Are you ready to break free from your pain cycle and TAKE BACK YOUR POWER? If you are ready to take charge of your recovery, then please contact me to schedule a free 30-minute Take Charge Session at seema@seemagiri.com

> *"There is no greater gift you can receive than to honor your calling. It's why you were born and how you become most truly alive."*
> **— Oprah Winfrey**

Thank You!

The Modern Healer

HERMAN SIU
& MARTIN SIU

Good health is a God-given right; it's our birthright. Yet, while we have made huge technological advances to facilitate cross-planet communication in real-time, we haven't been as progressive in keeping ourselves healthy.

We may be living longer but, tragically, children are dying from cancers, diabetes is on the rise, and young adults are suddenly getting heart attacks. Chronic fatigue, depression, and anxiety assail us. We rely on drugs to fix our health problems and we spend billions of dollars on prescriptions that may alleviate the symptoms but leave the root cause untouched. In our fast-paced societies, we have lost the connection with nature and the natural elements that make up our bodies. Surely, there is an alternative way to heal ourselves, or even to prevent disease from occurring in the first place.

The long and short of it is that we don't have to drop out of society and reside in the woods to live happier and healthier lives. The answer to good health and longevity lies right at our fingertips – in the air we breathe, the foods we eat, and water we drink. That's the best prescription for the Modern Healer, and these are the guiding principles we use in our healing practice. As 5th and 6th generation healers immersed in traditions that date back to ancient Chinese Shaolin practices, we adhere to the disciplined and holistic approach of our forefathers.

We believe that a body in full balance has everything it needs to fight off disease, stay and look young, and be active and involved, regardless of the biological age. This belief has been supported by patient outcomes through successive centuries of practice by the healers in our family. We share this knowledge with you to empower you as a Modern Healer, so that you may take control of and assume responsibility for your own health and be the expert in your own healing and wellness journey.

To be empowered as a Modern Healer, you must first understand the core concepts of energy or Qi (chi) as defined by ancient Chinese healing texts.

Dr. Paul Unschuld, a highly-regarded authority on Chinese medicine and multi-book author said, "The core Chinese concept of qi bears no resemblance to the Western concept of 'energy'. We perceive that there is a knowledge gap in the current understanding of eastern medicine in the western world. Mindful of the wisdom suggested by the Chinese proverb, "A journey of a thousand miles begins with a single step," we have written this chapter as our first step towards bridging that divide.

There are three primary components to balance Qi. Qi is a fundamental power underlying all of nature, and it is a vital life force that runs through our body. There are three primary components to balance our Qi. The first component to boosting our Qi is the air we breathe, the second is the food we eat, and the third is the water we drink.

AIR GIVES LIFE

Almost all of life needs oxygen to survive. We take in oxygen from our surroundings to harness energy and use it to power the inner workings of our bodies.

In the Huangdi Neijing, the ancient Chinese foundation medical text, the lungs breathe in what's known as, da qi, or "great qi.". Once we breathe in the air, the lungs extract the Qi from the da qi. Based on this understanding, we perceive that Qi relates to life-sustaining oxygen.

What is the secret to having great Qi? It is the harmonization of the mind, body, and spirit.

In martial arts, we use our mind to harness Qi by controlling our breath. We use our body to breathe, and we put our bodies through constant practice to master our Qi. Once it has been mastered, the Qi can be at our fingertips in a moment's notice. We call it in this form the spirit.

Viewed from this perspective, it's simple to make the most of living and get the best use of your life. The first step to taking back control of your health is by learning to breathe correctly.

Notice, right this moment, how you are breathing. Are you breathing from your diaphragm or the stomach, or are you taking in quick snatches of air? The majority of us take shallow breaths because we have forgotten how to breathe deeply and fully, and the only time we do so is when we are in yoga or meditation. Having become a society of superficial breathers, we are not benefitting from the fact that 70% of the toxins in our bodies are released through breath. By breathing shallowly, we are shortchanging ourselves because hypoxia, or insufficient oxygen in the body's cells, has been linked to degenerative diseases.

Remember, breath equals life and a long breath enhances a long life. Breathing correctly is your first responsibility as a Modern Healer.

FOOD FOR HEALING

The second primary component to balance our Qi is food.

The ancient Greek physician, Hippocrates, who is widely known as the "Father of Medicine", is quoted as saying "Let food be thy medicine and medicine be thy food." Fast forward several centuries; Dr. Roger J. Williams, who discovered the B-vitamin, said in 1971, "The human body heals itself and nutrition provides the resources to accomplish the task." The Chinese are well known to eat their food in its season. For example, no watermelon is eaten in winter since it grows in the hot summer climate.

It is empowering to discover that we need look no further than our own gardens and our kitchens to find healing nutrition that supports health for our family. By making healthy food choices, we ensure that we age gracefully and live out the rest of the twilight years harmoniously and peacefully, without the blight of Alzheimer's, dementia, or other failing diseases.

"So many people spend their health gaining wealth & then have to spend their wealth to regain their health." - Chinese proverb

Our philosophy is that, with right air, right food and right water (in this order), you detoxify naturally, without having to go on rigid short-term fasts.

With the right balance of foods that are appropriate to your body type, you'll get rid of excess fat and flab, find the correct body weight, be brimming over with energy, have the mental clarity to solve challenges with ease, and be in love with your life.

If you're tired of feeling frustrated, angry, depressed, unsure, overweight, tired, and in despair, look to your shopping list, refrigerator and kitchen closets for the culprits. Are they full of processed foods and refined sugars? Are you eating natural grains, green leafy vegetables and fresh fruit?

In this chapter, we'll draw on healing secrets that we share with our clients in our Toronto-based clinic. We'll discuss the major foods that prevent inflammation, help you recover from cuts and wounds, and help detoxify the system.

But for the Modern Healer, the first line of defense is maintaining a healthy pH balance. Acid is corrosive and is the biggest culprit of many degenerative and deadly diseases. It's true that some acid is needed in the body. The stomach uses it to break down the food we eat into macronutrients such as proteins, fats and carbohydrates, and micronutrients such as vitamins and minerals that it may be easily absorbed by the body. But most typical diets are packed with sugar, animal proteins, and processed foods.

WHY PH BALANCE IS CRUCIAL TO GOOD HEALTH

The pH is a measure of acidity or alkalinity. The billions of cells that make up our bodies need an alkaline environment to function, to stay healthy, and to regenerate. Too much acid in our bodies creates ripe conditions for the growth of bacteria, yeast, fungus, viruses, mold and other diseases. Cells that are starved of oxygen are unable to regenerate. Once starved, they are unable to repair damage or rid the body of noxious chemicals and toxins. In time, the cells die; research now points out that cancer is the result of an over-acidic body. An ideal balance for our bodies is measured between a pH of 7.2 – 7.4. You can measure this by dipping pH testing strips into a sample of saliva or urine. An acidic body will produce a pH reading of less than 7.2, which means there is a lack of oxygenation at the cellular level. Your body may even create more fat cells to store the corrosive acid, leading to unwanted weight gain. If the body is malnourished or lacking any Alkaline minerals, it goes in search of calcium to optimize the pH level, and extracts calcium from your bones (joints), teeth and tissues which in turn leaves the bones weak. Calcium is one of the most important alkaline minerals as it increases the oxygen level in the blood. This calcium depletion results in arthritis and osteoporosis. In the initial stages of over-acidity, you may suffer from joint pains, headaches, and weight gain. In an acidic state, the body is trying to expel excess acid through your skin, causing muscle cramps, eczema, acne, swelling, irritation, and general aches and pains. People in this state get grouchier and irritable, and they age faster than those with a balanced pH body. Other so-called modern diseases linked to an acidic body include diabetes, osteoarthritis, acid reflux, irritable bowel syndrome, premature aging, muscle and chronic fatigue, bone loss and osteoporosis.

"The only way to keep good health is to eat what you don't want, drink what you don't like, & do what you'd rather not" -Chinese proverb

GETTING YOUR PH BALANCE RIGHT THROUGH FOODS

Our experience has shown that a balanced diet should be 85-90% alkaline and 10-15% acidic. Body functions and hand-eye coordination work at their optimal state at these levels. It's better for the body to be slightly alkaline than it is to be slightly acidic. Now that we understand why the pH balance is the first line of defense and why it's crucial to maintain the correct pH balance, let's explore quickly what foods contribute to a more alkaline state and more acidic state. A food is classified as alkaline or acidic according to its mineral content. Alkaline-forming foods contain more minerals such as calcium, magnesium, manganese, iron, and potassium. Some acid-promoting minerals include phosphorous, copper, and sulfur. Carbonated drinks are acid forming because they are loaded with sugar and phosphorus, which can lead to weight gain. Have a healthy serving of kale or broccoli instead, which nourishes your body with helpful calcium and magnesium for bone and muscle health. Alkaline foods include apples, apricots, cantaloupes, cauliflower, broccoli, kale, almonds, chestnuts and walnuts. The complete list is much longer and we will examine the healing qualities of alkaline-based nutrition in the section under Anti-Inflammation Foods. Acidic foods include ice-cream, manufactured processed foods with refined sugar, meat, fish, poultry, and eggs. This is not to say that all fruits and vegetables are alkaline. Some are in fact very acidic. Acidic vegetables include corn, onions, and garlic. In the fruit category will fall cranberries, blueberries, and currants. As you grow older, it's harder to expel the acid that is in your body. The longer acid exists, the more it will congeal and the more it will attack your cells and immune system. Acidic conditions manifest one illness at a time. Symptoms include arthritis, muscle fatigue, and body aches. At the point that you are weakest is when you're most prone to infections and diseases because infections live off acidic waste products. At our clinic, we will examine the root cause of your health problems, not just the symptoms. We will customize a holistic healing plan drawing on our experience and expertise to restore you to the right balance, homeostasis, so you may live your life in joy and harmony.

> *"Tell me and I'll forget; show me and I may remember; involve me and I'll understand"* - Chinese proverb

ALKALINE AND ANTI-INFLAMMATION FOODS

Inflammation is a natural body response to injury. You bruise when you hit your shin against a table leg or when you sprain an ankle. Chronic inflammation, if undetected, can result in debilitating illnesses such as heart disease, cancer, diabetes, arthritis, and Alzheimer's. Fried and processed foods, as well as foods that contain trans-fat, increase the risk of inflammation. We've mentioned that alkaline foods prevent inflammation, and these are ordinary fruits, vegetables, and herbs that you can find in your refrigerator, spice cabinet, and even in your own garden. There are many creative ways to prepare these foods for a delicious, nutritious, beneficial anti-inflammation diet/alkaline diet. Here is a small list of foods to keep your body in balance and in good health.

Avocados: they contain healthy fats, phyto-proteins, vitamins, minerals and dietary fiber that is sorely lacking in the western societies. Low in sugar content, avocados may help to lower cholesterol levels, and increase resistance to diabetes, coronary heart disease, stroke and cancer, while promoting a healthy body weight and body mass index (BMI). Avocados are best eaten fresh.

Bamboo shoots: which is not a common vegetable on the western table, were identified by the Compendium of Materia Medica, the most comprehensive medical book in the history of traditional Chinese Medicine. Bamboo shoots promote the circulatory system, supplementing the body's natural energy, and are recommended as a daily dish. A traditional forest vegetable in Chinese diets for 2,500 years, nutrient-rich bamboo shoots are being shown in modern research to help prevent cancer, and to aid in weight loss, digestion, and the appetite.

Bamboo shoots are rich in essential amino acids and fatty acids and, because of their low sugar content, they are useful for treating hypertension, hyperlipemia, and hyperglycemia.

Broccoli: just about all vegetables are good, but some are more alkaline than others. Broccoli counts among the latter as it is rich in important vitamins such as A, C, K, B-complex and minerals including iron, zinc, and phosphorus. Broccoli is also rich in phytonutrients, which are natural chemicals that help protect plants and prevent disease in our bodies.

Broccoli helps to prevent osteoarthritis, reduces the risk of cancer, and has been shown to help reverse diabetes and heart damage. Broccoli is best lightly steamed or gently stir-fried; overcooking will neutralize its benefits.

Cabbage: A source of Vitamins K, C, B6, folate, and thiamine. Cabbage is also a source of iodine to support the health of the brain and the nervous system. This vegetable, which is a staple in Chinese kitchens around the world, helps to lower cholesterol and is rich in glucosinolates that are shown to have cancer prevention properties.

Carrot: Raw or cooked, carrots are a rich source of Vitamins A and C, calcium and iron, and the anti-oxidant beta-carotene that gives the vegetable its orange colour. In addition, carrots contain fibre, Vitamins K and E, potassium, folate, manganese, magnesium, zinc, and some phosphorus. Carrots improve our vision, delay aging, help with regulating blood sugar, improve digestion, and help prevent cancer. There is a side note to add: overconsumption of carrots can be toxic so, if you start turning orange, you may want to cut back on your carrot intake!

Cauliflower: The cauliflower is packed with vitamins such as B1, B2, B3,

B5, B6, B9, C and K, as well as being rich in omega 3, fatty acids, fibre, manganese, and potassium. Apart from delivering powerful antioxidants, cauliflower is a healthy source of protein and fibre, it enhances the body's ability to detoxify, reduces the risk of inflammation and the incidence of cancer. Cauliflower is best lightly cooked through a simple sauté.

Spinach: Spinach is widely acknowledged to be rich in vitamins and minerals such as magnesium, iron, copper, calcium, potassium, and zinc. The dark green spinach is packed with anti-oxidants and health-promoting phyto-nutrients. If you're low in iron, spinach helps to make up the deficit. It is an aid in the management of diabetes, and works towards lowering high blood pressure and improving bone health. Spinach is best eaten lightly steamed, quickly boiled or sautéed.

Ginger: Mankind's historic cure-all, ginger is rich in anti-oxidants, vitamins and minerals, and also contains omega-3 and omega-6. Shown to be anti-inflammatory, anti-cancer, anti-nausea, and a powerful anti-oxidant, it greatly boosts the immune system. A versatile root, ginger can be chewed fresh, steamed, boiled in water to make tea, or grated and added to sautéed dishes.

The state in which it is consumed will affect its benefits greatly. Fresh ginger root fights the common cold, coughs, and asthma, while dried ginger root is better against abdominal pain, cold limbs, and rheumatism. If you were to use the fresh root for rheumatism, the condition will worsen but, fresh or dried, it is effective in preventing or stopping vomiting and diarrhea. Large quantities of fresh ginger are not recommended for those with high blood pressure, inflammatory bowel disease, ulcers, or intestinal blockage, and should be used sparingly if you suffer from gallstones. Excessive consumption can cause a person to break out in a rash as an allergic reaction and may also lead to heartburn, bloating, gas, belching, and even some nausea. From ginger root, we'll move on to alkaline-forming fruit and herbs to round up our short list of recommended foods. Remember, some foods are mildly acidic and some are weak acidic foods. Not all acidic foods are tarred with the same brush, but the worst offenders include processed foods, sugar, tomatoes, onions, garlic, dairy, and vinegar.

Apricot: the fruit and the seeds are effective alkaline-forming foods. Packed with iron and protein, apricots are good for quenching thirst and fighting asthma. The seeds from the bitter apricot heal coughs, sore throats, and constipation, as does the sweet apricot seed. But those suffering from asthma should eat only the bitter apricot seed, or the condition will worsen. Laetrile, a naturally occurring substance found in the kernels, has been increasingly promoted to help in cancer treatment. The apricot kernels have been documented to help fight against tumors as far back as 502 AD. The apricot oil has been used as far back as 17th century England to fight swellings, tumors, and ulcers

Peppermint: a herb with healing benefits dating back to ten thousand years in the past, peppermint is commonly used to fight inflammation. It soothes abdominal pain, indigestion, irritable bowels and bloating, and prevents nausea and vomiting. It is a popular healing food for the common colds that are accompanied by headaches, sore throat and thick phlegm. However, if you are suffering a common cold but have a runny nose, cold limbs and diarrhea, peppermint is not that effective. Although it is commonly thought of as an herb or a spice, it is actually cool and pungent, and should not be used daily. Those suffering from anemia or low blood pressure should use only as directed.

"Health is the greatest gift, Contentment is the greatest treasure, Confidence is the greatest friend, Enlightenment is the greatest bliss." -Chinese proverb

FOODS TO ACCELERATE HEALING OF CUTS AND WOUNDS

Skin is the biggest organ in our bodies, and we tend to take it for granted because small nicks heal quickly. However, there are times when there is a deep cut or wound from an accident or from surgery when extra support is required for the connective tissue to regenerate. Connective tissue is different from most other tissues because it is made not so much of cells, but from protein, notably collagen, fibres encased in a unique covering called a fascia. To boost your ability to heal quickly from cuts and wounds, look for foods with these four pivotal nutrients and minerals.

Vitamin C: Vitamin C assists in forming collagen to repair the connective tissue in the blood vessels, cartilage, muscles, and in the bones. Good sources of Vitamin C include fruits such as guava, kiwi, strawberries, and papaya. Vegetables include red and green sweet peppers, Brussels sprouts, broccoli, cauliflower, and sweet potatoes.

Vitamin A: Some of the foods mentioned in the category above will be useful for sourcing Vitamin A because they are rich beta-carotene that is converted into fully active Vitamin A. This vitamin serves many functions. It promotes growth, maintains the immune system, and supports vision. Other Vitamin A rich foods are sweet potatoes, pumpkins, carrots, spinach, turnip greens, and cantaloupe.

Flavonoids: These are a group of pigments that give plants their colour but are compounds that have been discovered to have anti-oxidant properties that are more powerful against a wider range of oxidants than the traditional antioxidants. They help the body detoxify, reduce inflammation, and prevent and reduce damage at the cellular level. Within this grouping, it's the flavonoid called catechin, which is found in great abundance in tea leaves, that is thought to inhibit the growth of cancerous cells. In addition to green, black, and oolong teas, flavonoids are also found in dark coloured berries, bananas, all citrus fruits, parsley, gingko biloba, and cocoa with chocolate content exceeding 70%.

Zinc: This mineral repairs damaged tissues and aids in healing wounds by generating proteins and other genetic material, boosts cell division andcollagen formation, and regenerates tissue, all of which are crucial to wound repair. It boosts the system, develops and activates the T-cells that fight off infection. Zinc is found in vegetables, nuts and seeds such as asparagus, bamboo shoots, Brussels sprouts, okra, potatoes, pumpkin, Swiss chard, lima beans, peas, pine nuts, cashews, pumpkin, and sunflower seeds.

KEEPING YOUR BRAIN HEALTHY

Fernando Gómez-Pinilla, professor of neurosurgery and physiological science in UCLA, describes food as a "pharmaceutical compound that affects the brain".

Studies conducted by him show that the brain is highly susceptible to oxidation damage, so foods that are high in antioxidants protect the brain cells from damage and dysfunction.

Omega-3 fatty acids: These fatty acids support the plasticity of the synapses in the brain that affect critical functions. These include learning and memory, fighting off depression, bipolar disorders, schizophrenia, and attention-deficit disorders. The particularly important omega-3 fatty acid is docosahexaenoic acid or DHA, which reduces oxidative damage, improves synapse plasticity, and is needed in the brain's cell membranes. Omega-3s are found abundantly in walnuts, avocados, flaxseed, chia, and kiwi fruit. Though typically recommended as a desirable source of fatty acids, we take a strong stand against salmon as a source of omega-3s. The oceans are filled with toxins such as mercury, dioxin, and more recently radiation, and seafood is filled with these dangerous elements. In our annals of healing, this leads to mental and neurological disorders such as dementia, Alzheimer's, and multiple sclerosis. It is much safer and healthier to find the fatty acids in nuts and fruit.

Folic Acid: The brain needs sufficient folic acid for its functions, and folate deficiency leads to depression and cognitive impairment. Combining folic acid with other B vitamins has been effective in slowing the rate of age-related decline in cognitive function, and in preventing dementia. Folic acid is found in green leafy vegetables such as spinach, asparagus, romaine, dried or fresh beans and peas, as well as in avocados, beets, broccoli, peanuts, sunflower seeds, honeydew melons, cantaloupes, bananas, raspberries, and grapefruits.

FOODS FOR DETOXIFICATION

In our view, a good detoxification is much more than a spring-cleaning. It's like a good oil change – you take out the gunk and replace it with good, clean nutrients that power the body.

We design tailored and customized detoxification programs that both cleanse and support your system. The concept behind our programs is that it's not enough just to flush out the toxins with a juice cleanse. Instead, you need to simultaneously put back nourishment and support that will revitalize and energize the organs and the immune system.

With that being said, the key organ that is most prone to work overload is the liver. The liver supports almost every organ in the body. It is the second largest organ in the body, and any alcohol or drugs taxes it severely. When that happens, the liver performs less than optimally, leading to an accumulation of toxins that in turn cause chronic illnesses. Natural detoxification foods and herbs are best prescribed after a complete diagnosis to know what is best for your body constitution.

Natural diuretics: Foods that flush the body of toxins are essential to a good detoxification or to counteract the effects of an unhealthy lifestyle. Among natural diuretics are watercress, dandelions in the form of tea, celery, and cabbage, in which is found the antioxidant glutathione to improve the liver's detoxifying function. Be advised that natural diuretics must be used with care; the amount and type to be consumed will depend on your individual body type and constitution.

THE TRUTH ABOUT WATER

The third component to balance our Qi is water.

Water covers 71% of the Earth's surface and is vital to all forms of life. Your body ranges between 50-75% of water as body composition varies according to gender and fitness level, because adipose tissue contains less water than lean tissue. Suffering from fuzzy short-term recall, having problems with mental math or reading small print? Those are signs of dehydration. Be careful in your choice of what you drink. Tap water, sodas, and coffee are all acidic. Our rule is 8x8. We recommend drinking at least eight 8-oz. glasses of water a day to neutralize the acid in the bloodstream for better metabolism and more efficient absorption of nutrients. For those looking for alkaline water, we prefer AquaHydrate, which has a pH of 9+, but only use as directed.

"*When you are sick of sickness, you are no longer sick.*" -Chinese proverb

BE AN EMPOWERED MODERN HEALER

We hope this journey into the healing properties of good nutrition will empower you to make the right choices. Whether it is to give you more energy, get you thinking clearly, accelerate recovery from illnesses, or to age with grace, the choice to eat well and live well rests in your hands. You may find the way ahead difficult and you may need a boost to get you started on the right footing. You may have inexplicable aches, pains, or chronic colds and allergies that just simply refuse to go away. Just changing your diet is not enough to get you on the healing path. Whether you seek preventative care or deep healing, we have the alternative modalities to help you with the healing transformation.

The body is a finely-tuned mechanism. It works until it is out of balance and, even then, it seeks to right itself until the imbalance has buried itself too deeply. Once it does, we are assailed with all forms of diseases and ailments, some too deep to be cured with just nutrition.

As practitioners, we tap into the secrets of our forefathers, into healing practices that have been refined and polished and provided to thousands and thousands of patients through six generations of healers. These are intricate and sophisticated methods of diagnosis, healing, and remedies that are the result of centuries of observation and practice that have withstood the tests of time and the tests of western medicine.

We are deeply immersed in a culture of healing and we drill down to the causes of disease and illness by identifying patterns of disharmony in your body. Our methods are gentle and non-invasive, and we examine not just the visible symptoms, but also take into account the subtle, intangible forces that make up all life. As healers deeply ingrained in a compassionate practice, we examine the physical, mental, emotional, and spiritual aspects because the body, mind, and spirit are inseparable. When you consult with us, you benefit not just from our knowledge and experience, but also from the cumulative wisdom and healing of our medical ancestors.

Martin and Herman are 5th and 6th generation healers steeped in Chinese healing traditions preserved through a lineage that dates back to Shaolin Buddhist principles. As father and son, they run their Toronto-based clinic on a mission to bridge the ancient and modern worlds to take healing to the next level. They seek to bring the body's energies to balance through a holistic and compassionate approach to healing. They customize nutritional plans and draw on modalities such as acupuncture and Tong Ren, a specialized energy therapy, Qi Gong breathing and exercise routines to empower the patient in the healing journey. They are currently co-authoring an upcoming book in response to overwhelming demand from their clients. It will be a thorough look at the beneficial properties, compounds, antioxidants, and micronutrients found in food, and will include ancient breathing and exercise secrets that assist in the healing process. Get more information at http://omaniclinic.com.

The Love Drug

Your Lifetime Supply of Metaphysical Pharmaceuticals

WILMA DAVID AGUILA

First of all, let me begin by saying I am an advocate of mental wellness and healthy living. In my sixteen years in Canada, I have been privileged to have worked in the pharmaceutical industry, innovating and developing drugs, and in pharmacies where I've had direct interaction with patients. I've learned through these interactions how wide a knowledge gap exists in regard to the awareness of the medicines we take. There's a gap with respect to what a medicine's focus and intention is relative to what the patient may want it to be. Interesting assumptions are made about what the medication may offer, sometimes beyond what the manufacturer intended, all in the search for normalcy and wellbeing.

I'm sure you know of someone who at some time or another resorted to the use of synthetic drugs to self-medicate. For example, some may use pain medications to deal with feelings of heartache or pain associated with failure, fear, anxiety or let-down. Sleeping pills may be used beyond treatment for insomnia, to deal with anxiety or stress. I've encountered people who believe an elevated heart rate that recurs has to be a symptom of a disease, when a little prodding reveals stress as the main culprit. Let's not forget the power of the internet, and how many of us use it to self-diagnose: perhaps the most detrimental factor that drives self-medicating.

The truth is that most people fail to listen to and put faith into the power of their inner voice and its influence on wellness and self-care. In this context, self-care refers to any necessary human regulatory function under an individual's control. There is no intention here to contradict the use of pharmaceutical drugs to treat a true condition or ailment as diagnosed by a medical practitioner, rather it's my intent to emphasise an awareness of metaphysics, and adopting it as a way of life. This chapter will explore a system that utilizes a series of phases to incorporate into your lifestyle and mindset that may be used to improve wellness.

We all have an opportunity to utilize self-care and awakening to help deal with things like depression and other mental illness. I have, many times, referred to an acronym I read once: C.R.E.A.M—Consciousness Rules Everything Around Me. It's part of the idea that we draw conclusions, right or wrong, from what we observe or are influenced by in our lives. If it's common sense to train our mind to focus on the positives and make it habit, then why are we not all doing it? It's also part of the idea that cognitive tools are often enough to remedy depression and other mental illnesses. Drugs should be a last resort.

Before we continue, I should tell you that my specialty is guiding people to experience the root meaning and cause of the problem(s) they are facing and to bring inner healing to the root emotions involved. My passions are focused listening, helping people with anxiety, and offering support and guidance in a loving and nurturing way. I also support women's health and act as a mental health coach to help those who are suffering with low energy, tiredness, etc.

Think about the metaphor of "moon phases." The idea is that we go through phases just as the moon does. Thinking of life in phases can help us to stay on track without feeling overwhelmed. For example:

- New Moon: this is a time to set intentions, choose new beginnings, embark upon new adventures and make positive changes

- Waxing Moon: now focus on growth, learning, creativity, healing and transformation

- Full Moon: complete the achievement of your goals, harvest what you have sown and protect what you have; it's also a time to focus on cleansing

- Waning Moon: open up, release and let go

Refer to and use the moon phases in your life to consistently reflect on the following ten steps to self-care: After all, the moon is a steady reminder that is always present and looking down on you from the heavens every night. Associating the moon phases to these ten steps is a roadmap to wellness and healthy living.

DRUGS

If you are someone who is troubled by drug use, the moon phase analogy can definitely help you. Before getting into the moon phase analogy here's a little background.

Misuse of prescription drugs is defined as the taking of a medication in a manner or dose other than prescribed; taking someone else's prescription, even if for a legitimate medical complaint such as pain; or taking a medication to feel euphoria (i.e., to get high). The term nonmedical use of prescription drugs also refers to these categories of misuse.

The three classes of medication most commonly misused are:

- opioids—usually prescribed to treat pain

- central nervous system [CNS] depressants—used to treat anxiety and sleep disorders

- stimulants—most often prescribed to treat attention-deficit hyperactivity disorder (ADHD)

Prescription drug misuse can have serious medical consequences. Increases in prescription drug misuse over the last two decades are reflected in increased emergency room visits, overdose deaths associated with prescription drugs, and treatment admissions for prescription drug use disorders, the most severe form of which is addiction. The percentages of prescription abusers seeking medical help is estimated to be in the double digits. Unintentional overdose deaths involving opioid pain relievers have more than quadrupled since 1999 and have long outnumbered those involving heroin and cocaine.

Now if you incorporate the moon phase analogy:

New Moon: make positive changes. First step is a desire to change. You need to believe you are at risk of jeopardizing your own wellbeing if you continue on this path. You need to believe there is a solution and a way out. If you could have done it on your own, chances are you would have done it already. Seek professional counseling. Find a branch of Narcotics Anonymous (designed with the same model as Alcoholics Anonymous), do whatever you can to reduce and eventually end your drug use. Change your focus. Look to substitutes for non-medicinal healthy substitutes to get you that high. Get high on life: it's the quintessential end, isn't it? What we're all searching for? If you aren't happy, look for the reasons why, jot them down, write what needs to change, set a plan to achieve it and, most importantly, work at it tirelessly. Make work and effort the substitute for the high. Bottom line… only YOU can do something about it.

Focus on growth, which is the Waxing Moon. There are many ways to overcome the negatives in life. A psychologist or psychiatrist can offer up cognitive tools or you can try some of the following:

a) Turn your back on darkness or negativity and look to the light. This can mean different things for different people, but the idea is to drive the darkness away, as dark cannot exist where there is light. Personally, I am always looking for the beauty in life. It gives me great joy. I find this beauty in nature, in art, and in the people I meet. I also have the good fortune of having the light of the Lord with me each day. The trick is to look wherever you can find something to lighten your mind and push away dark thoughts that can drag you down into self-abuse.

b) Consciously choose your thoughts and emotions. Life has no meaning unless we put it there. You have the free will to choose to think and feel what you want, no matter what is happening in your life. It's a simple choice that gives you great power. Choose yes or no, forward or backward, up or down, left or right, this thought versus that thought. Whatever the situation is, you can always boil it down to a single choice like good versus bad or light versus dark.

c) Emotion is a wild horse you must learn to tame and ride. Whenever any overwhelming emotion visits you, ring it in and ride it out. Sooner or later it will run out of steam and you will regain control. This kind of focus will take your mind off whatever actions you may have been contemplating when fueled by emotion. This approach will put you in idle mode while you take the wild ride on the stallion of your emotion. It's a safe way to deal with emotions that have the potential to harm. Emotions drive our actions, giving us the impetus to turn our thoughts into behaviours. Better to calm the wild horse and act calmly yourself than let it loose to wreak havoc in your life.

Harvest your efforts (Full Moon). Make sure you take the time to reflect over the past weeks and months to assess and identify where and how you've grown or changed. Celebrate these victories and record what has worked and what hasn't worked. Leap forward and complete some of the goals you have set. Now you'll have even more to celebrate. Reward yourself. Each of us has their own personal idea of what constitutes a reward. You may go out for a nice dinner, take a mini-vacation, or buy that book or movie you've wanted. It could be something as simple as stop for an ice cream cone. You are limited only by your imagination.

Waning Moon: open up, release, let go. Remember that even though you determine the right choice once, you may have to recommit to that same choice numerous times. It takes time to overcome habits and beliefs. The key to developing the long-term behaviours that are necessary for your success is to open up and let go of the old behaviours. You don't need them anymore, so dig them up and show them the light of day. Begin to understand that you are the source of all your thoughts, emotions and actions, and that this gives you complete control—if you are willing to take it. Remember that the drug behaviours are just that: they are behaviours you are choosing, not things that are happening to you. You can just as easily choose a better behaviour in this moment, in the next moment and so on. Eventually you will break the addiction—I guarantee it.

For personal assistance through mental health coaching, please contact **me@wilmadavidaguila.com**.

THE STRUGGLE IS REAL

Don't get me wrong. The struggle people with mental or physical issues have is very real and often requires the help of prescription drugs. The purpose of this chapter is not to deal with the current level of non-medical use of prescription drugs. Instead, I'm directing my words to those who are misusing legitimate prescriptions. These could be people who believe they are sick when what they really need is to learn some tough life skills, or those who began using for legitimate reasons but are now using for the sake of using. None of you deserve to have the small deviations from the set course translate into the huge monkey on your back. What is required is the offer of nonjudgmental help to learn how to deal with the underlying issues that have gotten you to the point where you are now. Psychiatrists, psychologists and some social workers can offer cognitive tools and other life skills to deal with what has, up until now, been dealt with by the misuse of prescription drugs.

The New Moon is a wonderful time to set new goals and make positive changes. To be a useful tool, goal setting must follow a set pattern:

1. The goal must be specific. Not "I am going to stop using drugs," but "I am going to stop using morphine within 30 days, beginning tomorrow morning and with the help of my doctor."

2. The goal must be timely. There's no point in setting a goal for three months from now. It needs to be something you can accomplish today. That's why you always hear about people breaking goals down into "baby steps" or "little bites." A goal is attainable by taking a certain pathway and then making constant course corrections to make sure you stay on that pathway. If a plane or a boat didn't use this same method, they would never reach their desired destination—because small deviations can take them many hundreds of miles off course. So … take on your goal by making many small decisions and actions designed to get you where you ultimately wish to be, today.

3. You must take massive action. Reverse engineer your goals into their smallest achievable tasks, then act upon them with great vigour. Take the shotgun approach: one shot covers a larger area so as to improve the odds of hitting your target. You can do the same thing. Take as many different actions as you can think of to achieve the goal at hand. Then do the same for the next and the next, until you get to where you want to be.

4. A goal should be something you're passionate about achieving. You can't get anywhere on an empty gas tank. Neither can you achieve a goal if you are emotionally bereft. Emotions tend to move us to action, especially if they are supportive or positive in nature.

The Waxing Moon is a time for focusing on healing, growth and transformation. The very act of setting and achieving goals will teach you and bring you growth. But it is up to you to use the things you learn so as to promote healing and, ultimately, transformation. You must actively focus on change. Why? People just naturally harbour change. It's in our DNA, going back to times when change meant injury or death. The problem is that, today, most change is not injurious. Change is actually beneficial in many ways, and embracing it often uncovers opportunities you might never have otherwise imagined. Focus on transformation. It's a good thing.

The Full Moon is marked by the harvesting of your efforts, the achievement of your big goals. Now is a good time to look at ways of protecting what you've achieved. It's also a time for you to wash away the cobwebs and begin choosing new goals. After all, if you're not moving forward, you're stagnating or even losing ground. If you're not growing you're decaying.

The Waning Moon is marked by the opening up of your mind to the new possibilities represented by the goals you've just set. You can release all responsibility about the decisions you've been thinking about. Now is the time to begin to move forward once again, drawing upon positive emotions only, and letting go of everything else.

I'm a great listener. For personal assistance through coaching, please contact me@wilmadavidaguila.com.

MENTAL ATTITUDE

Mental attitude is everything. How can I say this? Well, science has shown that the mind cannot tell the difference between what is clearly imagined and what is real. This is the reason why memory is subjective. It's also the reason why two people who have had the exact same experience may produce conflicting reports about the experience. What does this have to do with drug abuse? Using the concept just described, you can actually imagine yourself well! You see, whatever the mind of man can conceive, it can achieve. No truer statement was ever uttered. If you can see a thing in your mind, like a clear photograph, then you can achieve it. Your mind can't tell that it isn't real. Therefore, when you tell it to attain that clear picture, it will take you out into the world to find or create it.

New Moon: set that intention. Use questions like, "Can you build this for me?" When you get a "Yes," tell your mind to do it, to make it happen. It will listen and obey.

Waxing Moon: use your mind to transform the world and your life. Build something that never existed before you came along, or build a better mousetrap. Your mind is your secret ally.

Full Moon: Take what you have managed to do and protect it to the best of your ability, then rest and prepare to begin anew.

Waning Moon: Let your mind soar. Envision the possibilities as clearly as you possibly can. Prepare for taking new actions.

The topic of mental attitude also relates to one of the most important laws of the universe, the Law of Attraction. This law explains the impact of mental attitude. The Law of Attraction states that we will attract into our lives whatever we are focusing on. It is easy to be unaware of the impact it can have on our lives. Either knowingly or unknowingly, a person sends out thoughts and emotions and attracts back like a magnet more of what they have put out. If you leave your thoughts, emotions and actions unchecked it is easy to attract unwanted things in your life. However, there is also great potential locked within you, and if you apply the Law of Attraction in your life you can encourage the universe to give you great things.

One of the worst parts of misusing drugs is that the artificial feeling you can get from them encourages you to want to use them again to get the relief they give. This signals to the universe that you need more of the drug(s), and that is what the universe will return to you. The same occurs with misinterpreting medical health problems. The more you think you have a health issue, the more the universe tells you that you do. The opposite happens if you believe you can get better, or that you can stop using drugs. The universe will send positive signs, and as your health and lack of dependency improves you will receive more and more benefit from the universe. Focusing on your drug dependency brings more dependency, but focusing on the good in your life brings more good.

When you start sending the right signals into the universe, you have started the New Moon phase. Set your new intentions and welcome positive change. It is a new beginning. As the universe starts to return what you have requested due to the Law of Attraction, the Waxing Moon is in phase and the transformation begins. As your wishes and goals become true, you have harvested what the Law of Attraction and the universe have given you, and the phase reaches a Full Moon. Next the Waning Moon is upon you, and you let go, open up and think of the next thing you want to attract from the universe.

I can help you create more useful attitudes. For personal assistance through coaching, please contact **me@wilmadavidaguila.com**.

REACTIONS

Misinterpreted health issues and the drugs that follow rarely occur spontaneously. They are generally a reaction to something else. To get to the root of this you must inspect your life and find what is root of the reaction(s) that has led you to where you are. What is the stressor that is making you feel health affects and/or leading you to turn to self-medication?

Stress is an inevitable part of life, and completely normal. However, left unchecked it can wreak havoc on your life and happiness. It may arise from something as simple as traffic, an important meeting, or increased work load at the office. It can also be severe and prolonged, such as the stress experienced by those who have faced or still face emotional or physical abuse. When overwhelmed by stress, you may feel defeated, and this inability to cope may lead you to turn to unhealthy solutions such as drug abuse.

Not only is stress troubling in itself, but it can have real physical effects on your body. Physical symptoms can be vast, and commonly include increased heart rate, nausea, dizziness and digestive problems. What you thought had been ailing you may not be the physical illness you found in a book or on the internet, but actually a result of unchecked stress in your life. You may be surprised that some of the physical symptoms you face are healed by simply finding and resolving the source of your stress.

Deciding to find what causes your reactions is a huge first step in overcoming the issues you face. In the New Moon phase, you need to decide to make positive changes in your life. Your intention needs to be focused on finding out the cause of your problems and channeling your reactions in a beneficial way. During the Waxing Moon phase, you will grow and learn about yourself. Once you have identified what causes your reactions, you can transform those reactions into ones that heal you instead of just hiding your problems. As you feel the cleansing effect of constructive reactions you can begin to heal, and during this period you will be under the phase of the Full Moon. You will soon be able to open up, let go and release the baggage of your negative reaction (the Waning Moon).

For personal assistance through coaching, please contact me@wilmadavidaguila.com.

AFTERTASTE

When you first turn to drug misuse to solve your problems, they seem sweet. They appear to help you. You might even feel that your life has improved. What you will soon notice, though, is that drugs do not come without a bitter aftertaste. Focusing on this aftertaste is something you can use to motivate yourself to stop drugs and improve your life.

The New Moon phase is the perfect time to recognize the bitter aftertaste drug misuse leaves in your life. It is a time to learn that the drug may not be helping you as much as it seems, and may actually be bringing negativity into your life. It is the time to start on the journey of truly measuring the cons of your use.

As you learn more about the aftertaste of drug misuse, you enter the phase of the Waxing Moon. Your perception starts to grow and your view transforms from only seeing the positives of the drug to understanding that it also introduces negatives. This is an important step in the healing process.

At some point you will realize the drug misuse is just not worth it. This is the phase of the Full Moon. It is a cleansing experience, and the point where you see the drug for the burden that it is. As the Waning Moon phase begins, you let go of your dependency on the drug and open yourself up to a life free of the drugs influence.

I can help you beat your drug problem. Please contact me@wilmadavidaguila.com.

COPING

When someone is no longer able to cope with the stresses of life, they begin to look elsewhere for crutches to help keep up, or reasons to explain their failure to cope. Untreated chronic stress can lead to serious health conditions. These conditions include anxiety, insomnia, muscle pain, high blood pressure and a weakened immune system. This explains why some people improperly self-diagnose medical issues and turn to drugs for self-medication. It is important to realize when you begin to no longer be able to keep up and cope with life issues. Learning to cope with stress in healthy ways is an important aspect of a successful life.

Learning to manage stress in a healthy way, when it occurs, can mitigate many of the negative health effects it can cause. People are diverse and different and, thus, so are the ways they can deal with stress. Some people enjoy pursuing hobbies such as team sports, music and art, while others enjoy more solitary activities like meditation, walking and yoga.

I've listed below five healing techniques to help reduce both short and long term success...

1. Take a break from the stressor

It may seem difficult to step away from things like an important work project or a sick child, but when you allow yourself to do so there are many benefits. By giving yourself permission to have space from your stressor you gain the opportunity to do something else, and this in turn allows you to have a new perspective and practice techniques which make you feel less overwhelmed. This doesn't mean avoiding your stress completely, but even a twenty-minute break to take care of yourself can be extremely helpful.

2. Exercise

Everyday more and more research shows that exercise benefits not just the body but also the mind. While most of us know the long-term benefits of exercise, there are also short-term benefits. A quick 20-minute workout or physical activity during a stressful time can rejuvenate you, and improve your focus. This effect is almost immediate and can last for several hours.

3. Smile and laugh

Your emotions and facial expression can send feedback to the brain and have a direct effect on its function. When we are stressed we often hold much of this stress in our faces. Smiling and laughing is an effective way to relieve some of this tension and can improve the situation by signalling to your brain things are not so bad after all.

4. Get social support

If you feel overwhelmed, do not forget you can always call a friend or send someone you trust an email. Sharing your concerns with another person can help relieve your stress. However, trust is important, and you need to know the person will understand and can validate you. If your family is a stressor it may not help to share your work woes with them, and you may be better off calling a close friend.

5. Meditate

One of the best ways to help the mind and body focus and relax is to practice meditation or mindful prayer. The mindfulness that arises from this is a powerful tool to help you see new perspectives, and develop self-compassion and forgiveness. The process allows you to release emotion which may have been causing your body to experience physical stress. Just like exercise research has shown to relieve stress, a brief period of meditation can bring immediate benefits.

The moon phase can help you tackle stress effectively. Identify your stressor and plan how to relieve your stress. This can be thought of as the phase of the New Moon. As you implement your coping mechanisms and your stress begins to release, you are under the Waxing Moon. The Full Moon will signal you can cope with the stressor, and you can face and complete the tasks causing you stress under the Waning Moon without fear.

For coaching in coping and lifestyle skills, please contact **me@wilmadavidaguila.com**.

SIDE EFFECTS

One of the biggest issues with self-diagnosis and drug misuse is that people often only target the side effect. As mentioned before, stress can cause physical problems. Dealing with the physical problems may work temporarily, but the original issues remain. While drugs may make you feel okay, the true problem may still be growing under that shroud you have created, waiting for the right opportunity to reappear and wreak havoc on your life.

Don't assume the issues you face are the only problem. The New Moon is the phase of your life to search for things that may be causing the problems you face. Instead of tackling multiple problems individually and ending up leaving the root cause not dealt with, attack the issue at its source and deal with all the side effects simultaneously. Is your lack of sleep due to a medical issue or is it from the stress of taking on too much at work?

During the Waxing Moon you will discover the truth about your issues, you can learn about how the problems you face arose, and you can begin to heal yourself of your issues. Taking the previous example, you may choose to delegate some of the work. Your sleep might start to improve and you may notice you no longer need those sleeping pills. Additionally, you may see other side effects that you may have missed or linked to another problem. Now that you are not so tired you find yourself helping with the cleaning (for example) and causing less conflict with your spouse. These effects will leave you harvesting the benefits of the Full Moon. Once these side effects have stabilized you will experience the Waning Moon, and can open yourself up to new challenges and let go of the problems of your past.

For someone to listen and to coach you through your stress issues, please contact **me@wilmadavidaguila.com**.

METAPHYSICAL

Drug misuse isn't only related to physical issues but is deeply connected to the metaphysical nature of a person's being. Drug use can be looked at through a spiritual lens. Spirituality refers to belief in a power greater that oneself. One which governs the universe and has a sense of interconnectedness with all living things. It may also involve a quest for self-knowledge, meaning and purpose in one's life. Using drugs is a way to detach and disconnect from the present moment, and all the uncomfortable feelings that go with it. Drug misuse and addiction can also be thought of as having an isolating effect, one that can arise from a lack of connection to one's authentic self, a higher power or persons in the larger community.

Approaching the problems of drug misuse from a spiritual and metaphysical standpoint can be very effective.

One way to approach this is a metaphysical take on the 12 steps, from Ester Nicholson's book *Soul Recovery: The 12 Keys to Healing Addiction*:

1. You are the Power: Through my conscious union with the infinite universal presence, I am powerful, clear and free. Through the realization that God is within me, expressing as me, my life is in divine and perfect order.

2. Restored to wholeness: Through my conscious connection with the one power, I reclaim my spiritual dominion and emotional balance. I am restored to my original nature of clarity, peace and wholeness. I am restored.

3. Complete surrender: I turn my life over to the care of the God I understand, know and embody as love, harmony, peace, health, prosperity and joy. I know that which I am surrendering to, and I do so absolutely. Knowing that this power is the very essence of my being, I say with my whole heart and mind: Thy will be done.

4. An examined life: Through my absolute surrender and conscious connection to the one power and presence, I courageously, deeply and gently search within myself for all thought patterns and behaviours that are out of alignment with love, integrity, harmony and order.

5. Living out loud: I claim the courage and willingness to share the exact nature of my mistakes with another spiritual being. I am heard with compassion, unconditional love and wisdom. In this loving vibration, clarity, peace and balance are restored.

6. Honouring the inner child: I am now ready to release all thought patterns and behaviors unlike my true nature, which is wholeness. I free-fall into the loving presence of spirit within, and allow it to heal

every known and unknown false belief. I am transformed by the renewal of my mind.

7. Never give up: In loving compassion for every aspect of my being, I humbly surrender to the love of spirit. I know myself as a perfect expression of life. I surrender all, and I am restored to the life I am created to live.

8. Willingness: I acknowledge the people I have offended based on false beliefs, fear, doubt and unworthiness. I am willing to go to any lengths to clean up my side of the street.

9. Cleaning up the wreckage: Backed by all the power of the universe, I lovingly, directly and honestly make amends in a way that supports the highest good of all concerned.

10. Spiritual maintenance: I am in tune with my inner self. With integrity, love and self-compassion, I acknowledge my mistakes and continue to clean up the mistakes of my past and present.

11. Conscious contact: Through daily prayer and meditation, I deepen my conscious connection to the divine and experience the fullness of the universal presence as the dynamic reality of my life.

12. Loving service: Through my awakened consciousness, I am now prepared to carry the message of truth out into the world. I am now a clear channel to support the awakening of others to their true identity of wholeness.

The 12 keys or steps also span the phases of the moon. Steps one to four represent the New Moon. Steps five to eight represent the Waxing Moon. Steps nine to 11 represent the Full Moon. And the last step, 12, represents the Waxing Moon.

For spiritual and metaphysical coaching, please contact **me@wilmadavidaguila.com**.

VIBRATION

Vibration is your energetic resonance, and it represents how you think, feel and act. It is the energy the attracts every experience in your life. To ensure happiness and attract good things in your life you want to have positive vibrations. Keeping your vibrations positive will attract positive thoughts and in turn create positive experiences that will match the vibrations of health and abundance. Being in this state is a requirement to attract that which you want.

Dark energies and entities will weaken you and lower your vibrations. Drugs may be a choice you make to try to remedy the state you feel yourself falling into. Drug misuse may trick you into thinking you are improving but actually can bring your vibrations even lower and make a positive state even harder to achieve. Instead of drug misuse you should look into ways to raise your vibration and attract positive energy.

I've included ten steps that can help you raise your vibrations and move away from the vibration lowering temptation of drug misuse:

1. When situations or people drag you down, distance yourself from them so your vibrations are not affected by the negative energy.

2. Raise your energy and awareness by refocusing through daily meditation.

3. A warm bath with Epsom salts and a couple drops of essential oils can help you grow your vibrational energy.

4. Deep breathing is a good way to bring oxygen to your brain and blood stream, and allow your energy to resonate in a positive fashion.

5. Avoid the polluting effect of the toxins from unnecessary drugs, alcohol and nicotine.

6. Find ways to exercise creativity through things like art, poetry, writing or photography.

7. Say what you are grateful for out loud to help grow those vibrations.

8. Be kind to others in your daily activities, and genuinely smile to attract more of the positive energy that comes from it.

9. Exercising at least once a day can deplete negative energy and build positive vibrations.

10. Keeping hydrated keeps your body running efficiently and allows your vibrational level to stay stable.

In the New Moon stage, you need to focus on positive energy and the state of your vibrations. The Waxing Moon is where you will grow your vibrations by focusing on your health and creative outlets. As your vibrations grow you will transition into the Full Moon period and you will feel healing energy, and may even notice transformations beginning in your life. The benefits will start to become apparent as your new vibrational state stabilizes. This signifies the New Moon phase, and many new opportunities will become apparent. As you open yourself up to new energies and let go of negative energy in your life during the Waning Moon, you can prepare for bringing your vibrations to even greater levels.

For personal assistance with building up your energy levels, please contact me@wilmadavidaguila.com.

AWAKENING

When you begin to put the lessons from all the previous sections together, you will awaken to the idea that your personal issues or health problems are not always served by drugs. This point is the beginning of the overarching New Moon. It may take you many moon cycles to reach this place. As you learn to release all the various problems through past Waning Moons, accept that the issues you face can be fixed as you surrender yourself to the universe and all the good it can bring you. This Waxing Moon will bring immense growth and overall healing. You will transform into the best version your current self has experienced. The Full Moon will cleanse you and your wish for a life free of drug misuse will come true. The next Waning Moon will allow you open yourself up to all the potential that was already there but that you had not been able to see.

For personal assistance through coaching or for group seminars, please contact **me@wilmadavidaguila.com**.

Nobody Got Time For That!

The Ultimate Guide For Smart Money Management

URSULA GARRETT

Save, save, save! That's all you hear from family, friends and the media. You are strongly encouraged to save, but how are you supposed to save with a low-paying job, high student loan debt, and the rising cost of housing? Something has got to give – and it's usually not you giving to your savings account. Who has time to be broke when you are young and just want to have fun and enjoy your life? I'll tell you who – nobody. Nobody has got time for that, especially you!

Finances absolutely play a huge part in your life choices and opportunities. Money issues consume chunks of your brain power every day. Think of how many times money (or a lack of it) factors into your decisions throughout your fast-paced day. For instance, you schedule a date on Tinder, buy movie tickets on Fandango and make dinner reservation using Open Table, and you haven't even gotten out of bed yet to start your day. You can do this if you have money in your bank account or power (available credit) on your credit card. Yes, either method of payment will get you what you want right now – one is a smart choice and the other, not so much. You must make smart choices regularly, there is no getting around it.

Size does matter, especially when it refers to your bank account. I want you to recognize that money underwrites the type of life you live and the lack of it means you're not living the life you want to be living. You are forced to make hard choices about what you can afford or what you have to give up. Having limited options make you feel as if your life is less than it could be. Smart money management is the key to your financial goals and personal goals aligning.

Once you recognize that the choices you make with your finances are either limiting your options or providing you opportunities, you can start being more proactive with your finances. First, it is important for you to understand how easy it is to handle your personal business, so you can create real changes that will significantly impact your life.

Two of my five daughters are about the same age, 26 (not twins just a blended family). Throughout their lives, they have taken different paths and made different choices. They are in their mid-twenties now and both spend more than they should, however, one is contributing to a retirement plan and has money go directly from her paycheck into a savings account. The other one lives paycheck to paycheck, has no retirement savings, no personal savings, and is regularly subsidized by her parents. Three guesses which one has more opportunities to live the life she wants, and the first two guesses don't count. While they each had similar opportunities, their individual choices have dictated their current circumstances.

"I am not a product of my circumstances. I am a product of my decisions."
- Stephen Covey

It's a bit of a mystery why you make some of the decisions you make and that's especially true when it comes to your finances. I can tell you from experience that a crystal ball, mesmerizing though it may be, is not where you will find those answers. How often have you made poor financial choices in the moment, only to later regret them and wonder how you got into this situation again? Well, I'm here to tell you that it doesn't matter how or why, what matters is what you do to fix it and make sure it never happens again.

If you have ever paid attention to political elections, then you know how easily you can be fooled by your assumptions, fears and false intuitions. I say this to help you understand that listening to others' opinions about what you should do won't help you reach your goals. Making a plan and following through will.

Which is why I find it useful to understand some principle concepts when you make decisions about money. This is besides, of course, the regular practices of following a budget, saving, investing and avoiding most kinds of debt, factors that I will discuss as part of the steps for smart money management.

These four concepts are the foundation you need for your decision-making process when you are creating your budget or making the decisions about those investments and savings plans. They need to factor into all your financial decisions, because they will help keep you from sabotaging your financial stability.

1) OPPORTUNITY COSTS

No matter what you do or the opportunities that you pursue, there is always going to be a cost. You have to give something to get something. Nothing in life is free. Individually, we get to decide what we are willing to give in exchange. In some circumstances, the price is simply too high, or the payoff is too low to make the deal or take the chance. That threshold is different for everyone and is based on your values.

For example, deciding whether or not to pursue higher education is a decision you make based on your priorities, which could include your financials, your time, and your perception of the value of higher education. Pursuing an advanced degree may take years -- are you willing to put in that amount of time? It could involve giving up other opportunities to finish your degree, but at the same time, the network you build could allow you access to individuals who can create even greater career opportunities in the future. Many individuals choose their university based on the alumni and the type of network they can access for mentors.

Additionally, there is the debt that often comes with pursuing higher education. Are you willing to put yourself into that kind of debt, the type of debt that will take years to pay off? Many individuals see their degree as a doorway to career advancement in a specific field or as a way to pursue the type of work that they are passionate about. For them, the cost of the degree in terms of finances and time is worth it, because they see that degree as an investment in their long-term financial future.

Those two daughters I mentioned earlier, one went to college and has a degree in business and some student loan debt. The other worked part-time jobs and traveled to visit friends she met on the internet. One daughter wanted a college degree and was willing to sacrifice four years of her life, accumulate debt (she considered it as an investment) and forego immediate travel opportunities. The other daughter thought that price was too high. This isn't a matter of right or wrong but a matter of what you are willing to give to get what you want. Here is a general rule of thumb: The bigger the opportunity, the greater the cost or sacrifice to achieve it.

Every decision that you make has all those considerations and it is up to you to give them all a voice before you make your decision. At the same time, your priorities need to guide those smaller financial decisions that we all make throughout the day. Many of your long-term goals are going to be impacted by your short-term decisions. Therefore, giving yourself guidelines for daily spending based on your priorities will help you to reach those goals. Still, not everything can be quantified in terms of your return on investment, as I will explore next.

2) SUNK COSTS

What is sunk cost? This is money you can't get back -- a non-refundable airline ticket, for example. There are certain expenses that you will have throughout your life that are not going to bring a tangible return on investment. In fact, they are likely going to result in nothing more than an enjoyable experience or a pleasant memory. It can be easy to get into a mindset that has you spending far beyond what you may have budgeted or prioritized because you value the experience, but it can put you in a financial bind later. The idea here is that you need to keep sunk costs in proper perspective. It's easy to start thinking, "Well, I've already spent $100, so what's another $25?" My mother always told me not to throw good money after bad. She taught me to understand the concept of sunk costs long before I took a business class. You have got to be willing to walk away sometimes and keep the money in your pocket for other investment opportunities.

Once something is paid for, and cannot be refunded, it shouldn't impact your future financial decisions. It is a "sunk" cost, i.e. water under the bridge, and no matter what you do in the future you won't ever get it back. Therefore, you can't allow yourself to get hung up on the moments where you spent money in a way that didn't fall into your overall financial plan. In the end, you have to accept that sunk costs are going to happen and make your peace with them. Recognize that you will buy emotionally and defend rationally, even if that might not always be wise. There are costs that are simply not recoupable.

Regrets over sunk costs can make it harder to move forward, leaving you vulnerable to make other choices that you may not have otherwise made. Do not allow yourself to fall into the downward spiral. Negative thoughts often breed more negative thoughts, especially if you continue to dwell on them. The same can be said for financial decisions. When you focus on your bad financial decisions, you may find yourself repeating them, because that is your focus.

It is important to keep yourself focused on ways to improve your financial decisions and keep them in line with your financial plan. Yes, you might regret a decision, but make the conscious choice not to dwell on it. Instead, learn from it and move forward. Life, especially when it comes to finances, is a series of learning experiences. The better you are at accepting the lessons, the better decisions you will be able to make in the future. I find inspiration and humor in the lyrics of one of my favorite songs by Chumbawamba, "I get knocked down, but I get up again, you're never gonna keep me down."

Now that you have that mindset (and that song stuck in your head), you can keep yourself from making financial decisions based on your sunk costs and focus on maximizing your earnings. That starts by focusing on finding the right investments for you. With that in mind, let's talk about the Rule of 72.

3) QUICK INTEREST CALCULATIONS USING THE RULE OF 72

One of your biggest concerns about an investment should be, "What am I going to get out of this?" While you wouldn't want to ask that of a date, it's perfectly acceptable, in fact it's expected, to ask that of a potential investment. All of us want a way to determine the upside of a financial opportunity. Now there are several ways to analyze a financial investment, but it often comes down to how long it will take for an investment to pay off. Want to double your holdings? The Rule of 72 can tell you how long it will take, based on the specific interest rate. Just divide 72 by the interest rate to learn how long it will take to double your initial investment.

For example, if you are looking at an investment with an interest rate of 6 percent, then 72 divided by 6 gets you 12 years. You can then take that information and use it to determine if that timeframe will work with your overall financial plan. Granted, you may find that other factors will play a part in determining your return as well, but it is important to have an idea of what you can expect before you put money into an investment.

This is a rough estimate, of course, but it's pretty effective. Recognize that you might find that a return is going to take significantly longer to make you money. So even if you find it an interesting opportunity, you may opt to not invest in order to take advantage of a different opportunity that will give you a faster return on your money.

In fact, you can also turn the equation around to determine the interest rate you are looking at if someone promises to double your returns in a set amount of time. Twice as much money in 12 years? Divide 72 by 12 and you get an interest rate of 6 percent. This rule lets you evaluate investment opportunities quickly and decide where to put your money in a way that will help you to grow your investments to meet long-term financial goals.

Keep in mind, future earnings are not something that you can count on, so how you use the dollars that you have now are going to have greater weight than potential earnings. You know that old saying, "Don't count your chickens before the eggs hatch."

4) THE TIME VALUE OF MONEY

According to this concept, a dollar you receive today is worth more than a dollar you will get tomorrow. You will have opportunity to invest that dollar immediately and begin earning more revenue from it (and also avoid losing value because of inflation).

It is important to recognize that money from your investments needs to be put to work. Don't be quick to spend it. Making frivolous or useless purchases means you are making a choice to spend on meaningless things and activities and in doing so, you are draining your ability to invest and grow. Focus on how you can essentially create a chain of investments, all working to grow an income stream for you to use in retirement or even for a big purchase that is part of your financial plan (think a house or car). Growth is a long-term process and it is imperative that you do make the time for it.

When you are waiting for an investment to pay off, then you are waiting for your money to work for you. One of the ways that you can save money is by limiting your interest payments. When you are making money from investments, which is then reinvested, you create an income stream that can allow you to pay cash for items, or put down a larger down payment, thus helping to reduce those interest payments, or eliminate them altogether.

Again, this helps you make certain calls about your purchases -- and your income. It's the old "one bird in the hand is worth two in a bush" theory in action for your wallet.

These four concepts have served me well over the years. Now let's focus in on the five steps that will help you to remain financially sound as you invest and grow your income to meet your financial goals.

WHY MONEY MATTERS

Before I talk about the steps, I want you to understand that money has a place and purpose in your life. Whatever adventures or experiences you want to have, you are going to need money to do it. That money is also going to be a key part of fulfilling your life's purpose, simply because money is a resource that can help you get things done. Regardless of if your goal in life is to have a non-profit that helps others or to create a company to bring a product or process to market, the truth is that money will be a resource that you need.

Since you and I can agree on that, let's start talking about your financial goals by first talking about your life goals.

STEP 1 - BUDGETING: YOUR PERSONAL BUSINESS PLAN

You have goals you want to accomplish, experience, and create in this life. This is simply a reality we all share. By defining your goals, you are able to determine what financial moves are necessary to achieve them. Too often, personal goals are overlooked or under-appreciated when creating a financial plan. Your personal goals and your financial plan need to be in sync for you to be successful at achieving either one.

For instance, if you know that your financial plan is going to allow you to achieve your personal goals, then it will help you maintain the excitement and vision you have for your life. This knowledge will help keep up the momentum during tough times or difficult circumstances when you are making sacrifices.

Budgeting should be the first part of your financial plan, because it will show the money you have coming in and going out. Once you understand your cash flow, then you have all the information you need to make a sound financial plan. Your budget will allow you to make good choices about how you want to use your money and where you can make changes in your spending habits to align your personal goals with your financial goals.

As part of that budgeting process, you need to look at the choices you make on a daily basis. Consider that if you take out that Tinder date on Saturday night maybe you can't afford to play golf on Sunday. If you really want to golf, then maybe you have to Netflix and chill with $1 bottles of beer or a $7 bottle of wine and takeout pizza instead of your dinner and a movie date. We all have to make choices. Just make sure your choices are good choices. You may find that you are sabotaging yourself by the financial decisions you make every day.

The good news is that you don't have to try to figure out a budget on your own or hire a professional to do it for you. All you need is that device that sometimes acts as another appendage – your cell phone. Yes, there is another reason that your cell phone is your best friend because there's an app for that (for budgeting, that is). Actually, there are several apps for that, you just have to choose the one that works best for you.

I use Mint to track my personal bank accounts, credit cards, investments and bills – it creates a budget based on my income and expenses and reminds me when I have a payment due date. I love that my whole financial life is accessible in one place and that I can monitor activity at a glance. One of my daughters uses Clarity Money, which has similar features plus the added benefit of helping to cancel unwanted subscriptions. With an app, you won't have to wonder if you are spending too much money shopping or eating out, you can see it in full color. Knowledge is power, and this knowledge can be used to change your spending behavior to match your financial goals.

For instance, think about that $5 cup of coffee you stop to buy every morning to start your day. That money falls into the sunk costs pot, because you are not getting that money back and it is not working for you. Imagine how much money you could save if you took that $5 per day for a year and saved or invested it – you would have more than $1,825. Going back to those two daughters of mine, one likes to buy and play internet games, a lot – can you guess which one? I'll tell you it's not the one that uses Clarity Money. If you are having trouble saving to meet your long-term goals, then it might be worth exploring using an app to help you get control of your spending.

It is not about giving up your lifestyle, but making your lifestyle adhere to your financial priorities, instead of letting your lifestyle dictate your priorities. Everyone has time to know their money.

Part of achieving any financial goal is to create a nest egg of funds to work with, which serves as a basis for your investment portfolio. Using your budget, you can designate a specific percentage to go into your savings.

STEP 2 – SAVING

The point of saving is to create a financial resource that you can use to build your income streams. These income streams can be diversified, but the point is that saving has to be a priority in order to improve your financial situation and allow you to reach your goals. Here are just a few reasons why saving is important.

1. You have a nest egg for emergencies. Time and time again, financial emergencies have sunk individuals who appear to be doing well, simply because they had nothing to fall back on. Once it happens, they have a financial issue, one that can have a ripple effect across other areas of their lives. Point blank, having an emergency, such as an unexpected car repair or house repair, should not financially sink you. Experts recommend that your savings for emergency needs to cover six months of your living expenses. Once you reach that goal, keep saving a set amount to grow your emergency fund. If you have to use some of it for an emergency, then replace it as soon as possible.

2. You can save for larger purchases. You know that paying cash for items can save you money in the long run, because you won't pay interest on top of the purchase cost. When you designate savings for specific

purchases, it allows you to reach your financial goals without acquiring payments. Plus, once you make that big purchase, you can start saving for the next big item or event.

3. You can save to invest to build income streams. Once you have achieved your emergency savings goal, start building a savings that is specifically for investments. These funds should not be used for any other purpose, allowing you to adjust the rate of return to meet your goals.

Clearly, saving is important because it gives you a stepping stone to meet your financial needs and personal dreams. Now, I want to transition to the exploring the possibilities that you can create with a savings that was started for investing.

STEP 3 – INVESTING

When you reach the point that you have started an investment savings account, you have plenty of opportunities. From stocks and bonds to direct investing in a business, you have multiple ways to grow your investment dollars. That being said, it is important to choose investments that fall in line with your goals and your risk tolerance level.

For instance, if you are at the beginning of your career, you might find yourself more inclined to look for high return, risky investments. Why? Many of those who are younger see time on their side and recognize that they have time to recover from a loss. Alternately, as you reach specific benchmarks or get closer to achieving your financial goals, you will start to make less risky investments.

Another potential scenario is that you are planning to get married or start a family, in which case, you might be more concerned with the risk of losing the primary financial provider. In a case like this, you may be more interested in investing in a disability or life insurance policy or even starting a college fund. After all, not all investments are created equal.

Where you are in your life can play a large part in what type of investments you choose to take on. Additionally, you might take on investments that are less time-consuming because they give you the ability to do more of what you enjoy. On the other hand, you might want to be more hands-on in your investments, so that may be a factor in the types of investments you choose.

Your investment plan should be personalized to you and designed to meet your needs. I want you to recognize that working with a financial advisor can help you to determine the best investments for you.

Many of the individuals I work with even consider investing in themselves, which means starting their own business. If you want to explore your entrepreneurial spirit, that can be a great way to invest and see your returns grow, using your investment dollars and sweat equity. Again, I encourage you to put any investment up against your financial plan. Ask yourself the hard questions about whether it will work towards accomplishing your goals. Doing so is critical to keeping you focused and on the path to achieving both your financial and personal goals. Just keep in mind that it takes time to grow and any time frames set by you can be changed, especially if the situation changes.

STEP 4 – AVOIDING MOST KINDS OF DEBT

Debt can drown you financially and make it difficult for you to achieve your financial goals. When you look at your budget, do you see areas where you are spending money on payments regularly? That is money which is not being used to create income streams or to reach your financial goals.

Be picky when you are choosing to take on debt. I recommend that you only finance things that will bring in money or pay for themselves. It's okay to finance your education because you expect your education to yield you a higher paying career. Do not finance your vacation because you will have nothing but memories to show for it. You can pay for your business advertising with a credit card but not your groceries. Avoid running up your credit cards, leaving yourself strapped with payments. The interest payments can quickly exceed your budget and be a drain. Use the cash in your bank account to pay for your living expenses because the interest on credit cards is usually greater than the interest you earn on money deposited in the bank.

Some debt can be beneficial and preferable because it shares the risk. I am talking about debt that involves investing. For instance, if you are building a real estate portfolio of rentals and you have $100,000 to invest, you might find that you choose to split that $100,000 into down payments for five properties instead of just buying one for $100,000. The reason is that you can increase your cash flow across five properties and they can also cover their own overhead. In the meantime, you are creating equity that you can tap into later to purchase more properties. The point is that you want to use your investment cash to maximize your income opportunities. Do not limit yourself because you want to avoid all debt – some debt can be good.

When weighing your debt options, be sure to look at interest rates. Do not feel as if you are limited to one lender or one financing option. Shop around and make sure that you get the lowest possible rate for your debt with the best payment plan to meet your investment needs. Also, make sure that any investment purchased with debt is going to have a positive cash flow. Some investments may not have a positive cash flow initially but will overtime as the debt is paid down. For other investments, it is the value which grows over time that offsets the lack of a positive cash flow.

Again, it is important to work with a professional who can help you determine what types of debt you want to take on regarding your investments and what debt you want to avoid.

In the end, this step is mostly focused on helping you to avoid debt that drains you financially, without giving you any type of return. Think about the cost of those daily coffees. The focus of this step needs to be on defining the lifestyle you want and then investing in order to be able to afford it. If you opt to live a lifestyle that drains your investments, you could be shortchanging yourself for the future, thus limiting your ability to reach your dreams.

STEP 5 – EVALUATE AND ASSESS: ONGOING PROCESS

I call this step, "the shit happens" part of your plan. Yes, it would be nice if life happened exactly as we planned it, but real life is no fairy tale. The reality is that you made a plan based on the life you wanted to live and all the messy stuff that got in your way is why you had contingency plans, emergency funds and cushions built into your plan. Shit happens, and you deal. You deal by adapting to your new situation. Update your plan as if it is a living, breathing organism.

For instance, you had an accident that kept you from working for six months. That would be both physically and financially draining. This is only a temporary setback. Now you need to reset your goals to achieve your plans, because you may need to focus on rebuilding instead of growth. Still, the point is to make adjustments that help you achieve your goals, thus not allowing the circumstances to overwhelm you and derail your finances permanently.

This need to make adjustments also applies to your investments. I recommend at least once per quarter that you review your investments to make sure they are performing as expected. You don't want to waste your resources on underperforming investments.

Are there areas you might want to expand even further, or do you need to eliminate some investments because they no longer fit your financial goals? Doing these reviews regularly can help you to keep your financial life on track with your personal life. When the two are in sync, then you will find that your life continues to improve. This harmony makes it possible to achieve what you want, no matter the setbacks you might occasionally encounter.

Keep in mind that evaluating and assessing will always be ongoing processes. The fluidity of life is that you can create plans, but events may alter those plans or even offer you new opportunities and experiences that you might not have even considered.

It is important to keep your mind open, both to new investments and to new experiences and opportunities in your personal life. They often can dovetail together more than you ever realize.

Financially, your world is built on the decisions that you make throughout your life. Always know the direction you want to go before you start your journey. When you make decisions without direction, your life will be like a boat without a rudder. It goes all over but doesn't actually get anywhere. The waves take the boat in multiple directions without a clear destination.

I want you to define your path and then work in harmony with that by making choices to complement it. Even with a defined path, it can be easy to make decisions that run contrary to your goals, as I discussed earlier in this chapter. When I work with individuals, I help them to not only define their path, but also to determine the types of goals that align with their paths. Then, I can help them to find the right investments and set financial goals to help them go further on that path.

Growth happens by learning from those people who inspire you to do and be more. We all have time to learn and grow.

Please email Ursula Garrett at ugarrett@cpagarrett.com or visit her website www.cpagarrett.com

Coping With Cancer

YVONNE ABOU-NADER

I vividly remember the morning of April 7, 2013. I had recently moved from London and was looking to buy a house in Chelmsford to be near my sister and her family. That morning, I was drying myself after a shower when I noticed a red groove underneath my left breast. An alarm bell rang in my head as I stared at the groove. I just knew, in that moment, that I had cancer. Until then, I never noticed the groove. I was not in the habit of examining myself because I never dreamed that cancer would happen to me. I stared at the red, grooved patch and my fears ran wild as I imagined the worst.

I lived with it for ten days while waiting for an appointment with my general practitioner. I was a mess during those ten days! Confused and anxious, I was not sleeping well and could not concentrate on my work. I continuously wondered how this could have happened to me. Suddenly, the importance of conducting self-exams to feel for lumps became all too real. My last mammogram had been four years ago; I should have had one two years prior, but somehow neglected to have it done.

I strongly encourage women over the age of thirty to examine their breasts and feel for lumps. If a lump is detected, diagnosis and treatment will begin early and there will be a better chance of eradicating the cancer and preventing it from spreading to other organs, increasing the survival rate.

I kept my discovery to myself because I did not want my family to worry about me. While waiting for my appointment, I went to Chicago for my cousin's funeral. Throughout the service, I kept thinking that my turn would be next. I was terrified! Each time I undressed, the alarming red grooved patch on my breast jumped out at me. Fearing that something that looked this bad would surely be the nasty type of cancer with a low survival rate, I worried that it would be too late for successful treatment and that I would only survive a few months. Again, I kept my fears to myself and did not tell anyone.

After returning to the United Kingdom, it was time for my appointment with my general practitioner. He referred me to an oncologist who did a biopsy and scan. Two weeks later, I went back for the results of the biopsy and scan. Sitting in the waiting room, it felt like an eternity before my name was called. As time slowly passed, my mind raced with thoughts that made me even more anxious and nervous. Eventually, my name was called and I followed the nurse to the consultation room.

The oncology consultant stood up to shake my hand, indicated my chair, then waited for me to sit down. I asked him what the verdict was. He said that although he had the results of my preliminary biopsy and scan, he would need to conduct further tests. He told me that, unfortunately, he did not have good news; I had stage 3-4 breast cancer involving the lymph glands. I would need surgery before they would know the extent of my cancer.

This hit me like a ton of bricks! You can imagine how a person would react to such terrible news. The words "you have cancer" feel like a death sentence. In that moment, my world collapsed around me. Confused, shocked, angry, and scared, I repeated, "No…why me? What is happening? Why?" My first reaction was denial, even though I had heard the words I had feared all along.

HOW COULD THIS HAPPEN TO ME?

I sat there in shock and denial. What caused this? How could it happen to me? I eat the right foods and do not indulge in junk food, sugar cakes, or fizzy drinks. I do not smoke and only drink alcohol occasionally, such as one glass of wine when I go out for dinner. I exercise and work 12 hours a day, while feeling fit and well.

Upon telling me the news, the consultant realized that I was in a state of shock and asked the nurse to stay with me. She took me to a room and sat there with me, allowing me to talk and recover from the shock. I kept on repeating "Why, why?"

What had I done wrong to deserve this? What would happen to the elderly ladies who I look after and the other charitable work I do? The nurse patiently sat and listened to me vent my worries and react to the horrible news.

Once I gathered my wits, she gave me a leaflet and explained that I could get help from Macmillan nurses who specialize in cancer care in hospitals and in the community. She told me there was a telephone number if I wanted to talk to someone.

Macmillan Cancer Support is a program in the UK that offers support to people diagnosed with cancer. They understand that cancer affects every aspect of your life and work with you to help you as you deal with cancer. They can be there during treatments, they can help with job and money worries, they will listen if you just need to vent, help with benefit applications, and even offer emotional support to your whole family.

(For more info, visit www.macmillan.org.uk. It is a wonderful resource!)

On the way home from my consultation, I fixated on finding out what could be the cause of my cancer. It had not sunk in that my general practitioner had told me to stop the hormone replacement therapy (HRT). I had done this for ten years to relieve the symptoms of menopause. I eventually did stop the hormone treatments. The other contributory cause was stress, which can be an underlying cause of many diseases and illnesses. My stress level over the previous five years was enormous!

I spent the next three days on my own, not saying a word to my family or friends. Instead, I bottled up my emotions and reflected on what I could do and what action I would take. I knew I had to deal with the problem and face reality. However, I struggled to think clearly or concentrate as my mind raced with fears and worries.

On the fourth day, I called my sister and asked her to come for a visit. When she arrived, I broke the news to her and we both burst into tears. She then phoned my brother to tell him the sad news. I spoke with him and he gave me his support.

After sharing my news and allowing others to strengthen and sustain me, I was in a better place emotionally. I knew I must be positive and do the right thing to overcome the anxiety and stress so that my body could fight the cancer. I made up my mind that cancer was not going to kill me, and I would beat it no matter what it took.

WAITING FOR SURGERY

Waiting is so hard! I felt like I had to do something while waiting for my surgery, so I searched online for alternative cancer treatments in different countries. I was particularly intrigued with how cancer is treated in Japan and China. I recalled seeing a program on television about a clinic in China that treated people with cancer using natural herbs. This had also been done in Mexico with good results. I discussed these treatments with my sister and brother, along with my niece, who is a doctor. All three did not want me to go this route with my treatment.

So, I continued to wait. The ten weeks I had to wait for my surgery felt like ten years! It was an anxious and stressful time. I imagined the cancer spreading further throughout my body while I waited. I feared my prognosis would become worse with each passing day.

I carried on with my daily routine and tried to remain positive. I went to the theatre, concerts, seminars, and workshops to keep my mind occupied. I also spent time talking with friends who were always supportive and sympathetic. I continued to work three days a week so that I could be around people rather than staying home and focusing on my cancer.

Finally, it was time for my surgery. I was nervous, of course, but also strangely excited because I was going to have this invader removed from my body. When I awoke from surgery, the surgeon assured me that he removed the breast along with 14 lymph glands from under my left arm. Two of the lymph glands were large and malignant; the rest were small and nonmalignant but were sent for further tests.

After three days, I was discharged from the hospital with a drainage bag in my side, which drained excess fluid, mainly from the lymphatic system. Once I felt well enough to leave the house, I carried the drainage bag in a concealed carrier bag. I was renovating my house during this time, so I went around to the shops and bought supplies for the people working on my house. I kept myself busy so that I did not think about my situation. Then I was notified of an appointment to see the consultant to start chemotherapy.

CHEMOTHERAPY AND RADIOTHERAPY

I was told that I needed six treatments at three-week intervals, then six weeks after the chemo I would need 16 sessions of radiotherapy. I completed all the therapies, but I regret them to this day. In hindsight, I wish I had followed my gut feeling to have the surgery only. The side effects of chemotherapy and radiotherapy are not worth having them done, in my opinion. Although I do not know where I would be today if I had not had them, I would not have done these treatments had I known then what I know now.

Chemo and radiation are akin to poisoning your system. They lower your immunity, killing good cells as well as the cancer cells, and some of the side effects are irreversible. I experienced all the side effects from chemo, including losing all body hair, losing my fingernails and toenails, nausea, vomiting, loss of appetite, metallic taste (even water tasted metallic), weakness, insomnia, a burning sensation, and pain and burning on the soles of my feet. I also experienced memory loss; I knew what I wanted to say, but it would take me a couple of minutes to remember how to say it.

Additionally, I had a chest infection and neutropenic attack that required admission to the hospital for four days. My white blood cell count went down to zero! I was given antibiotics and upon discharge from the hospital, I took Vitamin B and Vitamin C supplements. I am partial to Vitamin C for building my immunity and keeping me clear of colds during the winter. I also ate nourishing fresh soup I cooked myself.

By the third week post-chemo treatment, I began to feel better. The following week I had another chemo treatment and the side effects began all over again. I ended up having only five chemotherapy sessions rather than the recommended six sessions.

FATEFUL CRUISE

Six weeks post-chemo it was time to begin radiotherapy. This took place in a different hospital which was a forty-five-minute commute from my home. My sister took me to all my radiotherapy appointments and kept me company during the treatment. The radiation burned my skin and left a lesion on my body. The side effects continue today. I suffer from a weak heart and weakened muscles.

I finished the course on the twenty-second of December and on the fourth of January I went on a cruise! I took a supply of wound dressings and antiseptic to dress the wound. I needed to get away; away from doctors and hospitals and treatments!

I flew to Miami where I got on a luxurious cruise ship called Carnival Valor. It was a magnificent ship with 11 stories. Every facility you could imagine was on board. On the ninth floor there were many restaurants with a wide variety of cuisines from different countries. There were so many choices and many different offerings, from breakfast to lunch to dinner.

The group I traveled with and I were on the second dinner seating. There were many forms of entertainment with different shows each evening; live music, comedies, interactive activities, films and even plays. I did not feel like I was on board a ship; it felt more like a city!

There were over 3,000 people on board the ship. I was traveling with a group of 450 marketers who run their own internet businesses. During one of our activities, we each had two minutes to present our line of business, the method of advertising we utilized, and our results. We had fun exchanging ideas and getting to know one another.

This group did a lot of activities together when we went ashore. We visited Mexico and stopped at the Caribbean islands, The Bahamas, and St. Antonio. I met a lot of new people and made friends that took my mind away from my cancer. I enjoyed every minute!

One day I met another woman who had the same cancer I did. She had just finished her treatment and her husband brought her on the cruise to take her mind off her ordeal and to be among people. We had an obvious, immediate bond and enjoyed sharing our stories in a positive way with each other. It was so nice to talk with someone who knew exactly what I had experienced. We were literally and figuratively in the same boat!

After the cruise, I flew to Tampa, Florida to visit with a friend before flying back to the UK. I was so inspired after the cruise that, once home, I researched alternative treatments and subscribed to cancer research institutes and health science institutes. This led me to various studies and further research on natural treatments for cancer that boast an 80-95% success rate.

MY LIFESTYLE CHANGES

I changed my diet completely and chose to follow Dr. Budwig's diet. I cut down on eating chicken, turkey, and dairy products (except for cottage cheese). I had not eaten red meat since 1986, but in the Budwig Diet you can have red meat every now and then, provided the animal is grass-fed. I continued to carry on eating freshly ground flax seeds, either with vegetable soup or mixed with quark or cottage cheese.

I also began making my own vegetable juices, using mainly organic spinach, kale, carrots, and lettuce. I ate a lot of salads and fresh fruits, including many berries: blueberries, raspberries, strawberries, and black currants. I also eat a lot of red grapes, apples, apricots, and red plums.

I bought lots of books and articles on published research about natural treatments that use diet. I have since met many people who are alive and have been cancer free for 20 years who eschewed chemo and radiation in favor of using their diet as treatment. This is, of course, a personal choice for each individual to make as each person's experiences, treatments, and outcomes will be different.

In addition to the changes I mentioned, I also eliminated sugar and artificial sweeteners; instead, I use natural stevia. I avoid many starches and carbohydrates, eating only small amounts of whole grain breads and pastas. I suggest that you avoid ready-made meals as they are usually full of preservatives. I also recommend that you avoid genetically modified foods and conventionally processed meats as the animals are often given antibiotics and fed dried foods with chemicals. I fear that these additives could cause cancer. Instead, I choose to serve fresh vegetables and organic chicken, fish, or beef.

I have since made long-term changes to my diet because I believe it may prevent my cancer from occurring again. I recently became a vegetarian and I am loving it!

In addition to diet changes, I employed other lifestyle changes as well. I try to avoid stress and worrying. That is much easier said than done! I remember how stressful it was when I discovered the mark on my breast and then later when I heard that I had cancer. Most people will remember how they felt when they were told they have cancer.

Each one of us experiences similar feelings, but each one has his or her own method for dealing with the stress and anxiety, particularly those with young children. You may experience many different emotions during your cancer diagnosis, treatment, and recovery. You may be frightened about what the future will bring to you and the effect it will have on your family. You may feel shocked and angry, as I did, but relieved to know that there is treatment available. If cancer is found and treated early, it may not be the end of your life.

There is much enjoyment to be had in life after cancer treatment. Be positive and think of a bright future ahead of you. Enjoying life to the fullest will help your progress. Have faith and believe that you will conquer cancer and live a normal life!

STRESS, DEPRESSION, AND ANXIETY

It is natural to have feelings of anxiety and/or depression when you are coping with a potentially life-threatening illness. It would be strange if you did not have these feelings! It is how you deal with it that is so important; each one of us has a way to cope with the stress and anxiety.

Anxiety can have many physical and emotional effects, from irritability, moodiness, mood swings, difficulty making decisions, memory loss, fatigue, depression, loss of appetite, and insomnia. Physical signs can include muscle tension, tightness in the chest, a racing heartbeat, and hyperventilation. When these symptoms occur simultaneously, it is called a panic attack.

I experienced most of these during my cancer treatment, but I did my best to prevent anxiety from having a drastic effect on me. I believe the cause of my cancer was the stress I had over the years before the cancer appeared. Today, I do my best to avoid any stress, which is sometimes difficult.

Stress may play a role in the onset of many diseases, particularly cancer, heart problems, and mental illnesses. Stress may reduce your life expectancy and may damage your relationship with your partner and people around you. Anxiety and stress are emotionally devastating and can lead to long-term mental illness. A study published by the American Medical Association in 2008 revealed that anxiety and stress, left untreated, can impair key areas in the brain and cause the symptoms I mentioned above. When we are stressed there will be a shortage of serotonin and Gaba compound in the body. These compounds are the body's natural anxiety and stress relievers, acting as a speed limit for the frenzied communication in the brain. Ignoring stress by brushing it under the rug and hoping it will go away on its own will not work.

When you find that anxious thoughts are taking over and preventing you from focusing on your daily life or affecting your relationship with your loved ones and the people around you, then you need to seek the help of professional people. Do not blame yourself, it is not your fault; many people feel this way. If this happens, you need to seek help from professional people. Ask your doctor to refer you to a counseling service. Most of the time it is easier to talk to a counselor rather than your family and friends. You can tell the counselor exactly how you feel without a filter and they will listen and show you empathy. They will be able to ask questions, perhaps to recall a happy memory or event, to distract you from your negative thoughts and put a smile on your face. Over time this can change the state of your mind by interrupting the negative patterns. to.

Your doctor may suggest antidepressants. I do not accept antidepressants for long-term usage. I believe that they are okay for short term usage, as you are going through a particularly stressful event, but they can be addictive and sometimes cause suicidal thoughts. There is no medical cure for anxiety or depression, only treatments. I believe you need to seek help from a qualified counselor, consider altering your diet, and make changes to your lifestyle.

TIPS FOR COPING WITH STRESS

If you continue to worry about the cancer coming back, your body may produce the same kind of stress hormone as if this were really happening. These stress hormones can cause your mind to be more anxious which results in a vicious cycle that can be difficult to break. There are several things you can do for yourself to cope with stress in addition to seeking professional help. Many of the following suggestions are simple things you can easily do for yourself, yet many of us never think of doing them. I hope you will refer to this list anytime you are feeling anxious, stress, or depressed.

- **Find a hobby:** First of all, it is important to have a healthy distraction, such as a hobby. If you do not currently have a hobby you enjoy, find one! Think of things that interest you that you can incorporate into your life, such as painting. For me, while I am painting, I shut out all negative thoughts and feelings as I focus only on what I am doing.

- **Breathing:** When you feel anxious and stressed, sit down, and take deep breaths. Inhale and exhale slowly 20 times. Imagine each intake of oxygen carrying peace and serenity to all areas of your body. With each exhale, imagine all anxiety and stress leaving your body. Accept that you cannot control everything around you. Do not aim for perfection all the time.

- **Laugh:** It has been said that laughter is the best medicine. So, watch a comedy program on television or buy tickets to see a comic perform. Welcome humor into your life; a good laugh takes your mind away from your worries.

- **Avoid negativity:** Conversely, do not invite other people's stress into your life. Do not watch the news, especially late at night. If you have a friend or family member who brings stress to you, speak with them about it. Remind them that you are in treatment or recovery and do not need any added stress. Accept that you cannot solve the world's problem. Maintain a positive attitude as you replace negative thoughts with positive thoughts.

- **Volunteer:** A terrific way to fill your mind with positive thoughts is to volunteer in your community. Helping others makes you a valuable member of the community and gives you a purpose in life. Focusing on others takes the focus off yourself and your trials. You will feel so rewarded each time you do this!

- **Find a confidante:** Talk to a friend, family member, or even someone at work. You may find a sympathetic, listening ear among your colleagues. It may be helpful for a supportive colleague to be aware of what you are going through. Talk to a member of your family or a close friend when you need to vent about your feelings or your worries. Do not get upset if friends and family tell you to just be positive and pull yourself together. Keep in mind they are simply trying to help and are probably feeling quite helpless. They will not know how you really feel; no one knows except yourself.

- **Tea time:** Drink an herbal team, such as chamomile. In addition to the calming effects of chamomile tea, the ceremony of making and drinking tea will bring about relaxation. Once it becomes a habit, you may find yourself looking forward to your cup of tea and the relaxation it brings. Drinking herbal tea before bed may promote restful sleep.

- **Visualization and meditation:** Visualization and meditation, used separately or together, will reduce stress and tension, relax the mind and body, and improve wellbeing. Lie down or sit comfortably with both feet on the floor, inhale slowly to the count of five and exhale to the count of five. Focus your attention on breathing deeply into your belly. Feel where the breath is going in your body and notice the sensation of breathing out again. For example visualize yourself lying on the beach. Now add your five senses to the picture you have created in your mind. You see the beauty of the sun, sand, and surf. Spend some time here as you picture each detail of the beach. What are you wearing? How many clouds are in the sky? Are there palm trees nearby? Once you have a vivid image of what you see, move on to what you hear. Notice the sounds of the waves crashing on the shore and the seagulls calling to each other. You are breathing the fresh air and smelling the coconut sunscreen you put on your body. You taste the saltiness of the air on your lips. Feel the gentle warmth of the sun shining on your body and the coolness of the sand underneath you. Throughout the visualization, continue your slow, steady breath. Remember to focus on breathing deeply and attend to where the breath is going in your body. If you are feeling too overwhelmed to do a full visualization on your own, listen to a relaxation podcast, calming music, or a recording of natural sounds, such as rainfall, birds singing, or ocean waves.

- **Go for a walk:** Choose a visually appealing location you enjoy and go for a brisk walk. Make it a part of your everyday routine to walk for 30 minutes or more. It will keep you fit, helping your circulation and keeping your heart healthy. You will come to look forward to your daily walk!

- **Practice yoga or Tai-Chi:** Both Tai-Chi and yoga will improve your muscle tone, flexibility, circulation, etc., while promoting relaxation and a feeling of wellbeing.

- **Eat a healthy diet:** I know I have mentioned diet previously, but I cannot emphasize enough how important it is. Unhealthy foods, smoking, and alcohol can all exacerbate stress. Many people think these things calm their stress, but it is just the opposite! Additionally, an unhealthy diet may cause other health issues. Not all alcohol is bad. A glass of red wine occasionally with the evening meal helps you relax and makes you feel sleepy. Red wine is rich in antioxidants which are beneficial to your wellbeing. Do some research to find a red wine rich with resveratrol, a beneficial antioxidant.

- **Complementary therapies:** In addition to the coping strategies for dealing with stress, there are several other complementary therapies. These may be used alongside other treatments and include aromatherapy, reflexology, massage, music therapy, reiki, and acupuncture, to name a few.

A FAVORITE RECIPE

I have decided to share one of my personal recipes with you. This is the salad I have every day, with lunch and dinner, throughout summer and winter. I never get bored with it. I alternate some of the ingredients and buy varieties of lettuce according to the season and availability.

Yvonne's Herbal Salad

Ingredients:

- 4 leaves of lettuce (I recommend Romaine or whatever lettuce is in season where you live)
- 4 small radishes
- ¼ of a cucumber
- ½ small red onion or other onion
- 100 gm of rocket (also called arugula)
- 1 small boiled beetroot
- A few leaves of fresh mint or dried mint
- ½ freshly squeezed lemon
- 1 clove of garlic minced or chopped
- 3 tablespoon of extra virgin olive oil or organic flaxseed oil
- A pinch of salt

Method:

1. Wash all lettuces and vegetables under cool running water.
2. Chop the lettuce, radish, cucumber, rocket, beetroot, and onion and place in a bowl.
3. Mix the mint, lemon, garlic, oil, and salt together. Pour over the vegetables and enjoy.

Additions and Alterations:

Occasionally, maybe once a month, I add 40 gm of feta cheese to the salad. Other times I may add black olives. I sometimes change up the vegetables I use, depending on what is in season. I may use baby-leaf spinach mixed with rocket and omit the cucumber. I sometimes add a small tomato and grated carrot. I may use fresh thyme or dill, when in season.

I also like to add freshly boiled red kidney beans on occasion. I soak dried beans overnight and boil in the morning to use in my salad later in the day. (I never buy tin food, as it is full of sugar, salt, and preservatives.)

Other times I use boiled chickpeas in the salad. Or, I make them as a dip to enjoy on the side. I mash the chickpeas with added lemon juice, olive or flaxseed oil, garlic, onion, and mint. I enjoy this as a side with my salad.

I concluded that what you eat matters to your health to maintain your immune system and lead a healthy life. I hope you enjoy this recipe and that it inspires you to create other healthy options. If you would like to have more recipes and learn what to eat and do to remain healthy, build your immune system, and boost your energy, send me an email at naderyvonne@yahoo.com

Bringing Balance to Your Life

DENNIS GARRIDO

When I woke up in the hospital staring up into the terrified eyes of someone I cared about, after my second cardiac arrest in one year, I knew that things had to change in my life. Especially because I was only in my twenties at the time.

Everything in my life was out of balance. Obviously, physically because I was lying in the emergency room, but more importantly my mind, emotions, and spirit were completely out of whack, and that had taken a toll on my body.

Now you may be wondering how someone so young could have had two cardiac arrests before the age of 30? It won't be hard to imagine once I share my story with you. I wish I could tell you that I had a great upbringing, one filled with laughter and love, but it wasn't.

At age eleven I was removed from my parent's home by The Children's Aid Society because they deemed my parents unfit to raise me. During that time, I went through a whirlwind of emotions. A part of me was happy that change was finally occurring, because clearly at that point, the way things were, wasn't working at all.

Another part of me felt fear because of the unknown. I didn't know exactly where I would be living, nor did I know for sure what my group & foster homes would be like, what the other kids would be like, what the living conditions would be like, how far or close I'd be to my family and hometown, etc. Essentially, I wasn't 100% certain nor 100% convinced that I was going into better circumstances.

Also, I felt sad, since I wouldn't see my parents or siblings anymore, nor my home town and many of the people whom I'd see on a regular basis; everything FAMILIAR would be gone! Lastly, I felt angry, that it had come to me being removed from my parent's house, away from those who were in my life for all those years. As twisted and messed up as it may be, I was angry that I was leaving a life that I had become accustomed to and felt somewhat comfortable in (comfortable in comparison to the unknown that lay ahead); and most of all, angry that I was leaving FAMILIARITY!!!!

Please understand me, I am no longer angry at my parents, and you shouldn't be either. They did the best they could, but when you are broken yourself, unless you find a way out, you will repeat what had been bestowed on you from the previous generations. I can be thankful because what I went through helped create the person I am today and as a coach, it gives me great empathy and understanding to be able to help others. So, don't feel sorry for me because even though my life had a rough start, I get to choose the rest of it and it is going to be GREAT!!!

THE NEXT SEVEN YEARS OF MY LIFE

For the next seven years until I turned 18, I was bounced from foster/group home to foster/group home. I rarely spent more than three months at any one place, and it caused some major emotional setbacks that took me a long time to overcome.

One of the biggest negative emotional setbacks was again to do with familiarity. As I spent time with those at my new home, seeing them every day and coming to know them personally; I naturally formed a connection/friendship with them. It seemed that no sooner had I done that; they were removed from my life. People whom I really liked (a few of them, whom I loved), ALL GONE!!! Which basically solidified my already ingrained defence mechanism of keeping distant from others; not allowing anyone to get close enough to form any connection with me.

Inevitably, this made it very difficult for me to form any type of relationship with anyone. School and extracurricular activities were hard because I never knew how long I would be staying in one place. What was the point of making friends if I could never keep them? It was a lot easier to keep my distance than to reach out yet again and have everything torn away from me.

Eventually, I started to tear down the wall that prevented me from getting too close to anyone. To this day, the negative emotional setbacks I experienced, still affect me to some degree; though I CHOOSE not to allow them to prevent me from forming meaningful relationships!

THE DARKEST TIME OF MY LIFE

All that change led to one of the darkest periods of my life. Emotionally and mentally I had shut down and could no longer function. Life was so hard. Even things that were simple, now became agonizingly difficult and it hit the point where I didn't want to live anymore. What was the use of carrying on in this horrible life when there wasn't any hope of it changing?

My life began to narrow down to one permanent solution, and that was to end it all by committing suicide. I just couldn't handle life anymore, but I truly believe that Almighty God, the universe or whatever you want to call it, had a bigger plan for me. Even though I tried several times, I just couldn't die!!! Because of those attempts, I ended up in psychiatric institutions, a few times.

It finally came to the point where I was tired of trying to die, I was tired of institutions and I was weary from all the self-harm, and so I came to a decision. I guess you could say that it was a turning point in my life; I wasn't going to attempt suicide anymore. I wasn't sure what to do because my circumstances hadn't changed, but I was willing to look for options. That was the beginning point of change in my life. The will to live!!!

IT DIDN'T GET BETTER RIGHT AWAY

Life is a journey with twists, hills, and valleys of varying shapes and sizes, with occasional points where you make decisions that put you on a different path. The determination not to kill myself had set me on a new road, but I still didn't know what to do or which way to go. It was slow going as I fumbled my way through, but at least I was moving forward!!!

At age 18 I was no longer in the custody of The Children's Aid Society, so I moved back with my parents, which was the perfect testing grounds for me to apply the life lessons I had learned so far. You would be amazed by how much maturity one can have at 18 when you have been through what I have. It wasn't easy, and it was hard work, but I managed to re-establish a relationship with my parents and not only complete high school, but also graduate from post-secondary schooling.

One of the things I had decided to do was get my student loans paid off in the six-month grace period, which I managed to do; but in doing so, I pushed myself way beyond my physical limits which brought on the first cardiac arrest.

You would think I would have learned from that first experience, but I didn't, and less than a year later we are back to the beginning of this chapter waking up in the hospital from my second one.

This time I learned my lesson and chose a different path, but I still didn't know how to achieve what I needed. For so long I had lived in imbalance, that I didn't know where to start, but the catalyst for change was just around the corner.

I FINALLY REALIZED WHAT BALANCE WAS

Believe it or not, it is the simplest things that can bring about the most profound changes in life. My search for balance in my life had begun, and it is amazing how the answer came; by a knock at my door one day.

That day I was busy working on something, so when the first knock came, I ignored it. It was only after a couple of rings of the doorbell that I finally decided that I would answer it. There was a well-dressed gentleman at the door and even though I don't remember most of what he said, one thing became clear, I was missing an essential element to finding the balance I craved. Now, I knew what it was. You can only find balance when you address ALL the areas of your life, and I had been missing one. The spiritual side.

It is amazing what happens when you finally have all the pieces together. As I started to study the Bible, I finally could build a solid spiritual foundation, that enabled me to re-evaluate things in my life, and thus, put a plan together to create balance in my life. In the rest of this chapter, I am going to share with you what I learned.

Just before I do that, I do want to mention one thing. All of this is a process. Can I say that I am 100% balanced in my life? No, but when I started at 3-4% and then jumped to 85%, I think that is very good growth. It's difficult to attain 100% balance in every aspect of one's life, that is why even the most successful people keep learning and growing. So, the goal is not perfection, but growth. As long as you are continuing to move forward, that is all that matters.

7 STEPS TO BRING BALANCE TO YOUR LIFE

Here's one of the things that I have learned about bringing balance to your life. In some ways, it is easy. The steps I am going to teach you are simple to understand. The hard part is training yourself to be aware of it every day and live by it. The good thing is, though it may be hard at first, the more you practice it, the easier it gets.

STEP 1

Ask yourself, "What are my priorities in life?" You want to look at it from all aspects of your life, personal and professional. In terms of personal that includes goals physically, emotionally, mentally, spiritually, relationships (such as your spouse or significant other), family and friends. You want to look at it from the point of what you need and what you want. For each one, you should have one to two priorities.

In terms of professional, they can include your current work situation and areas of improvement there, plus plan for your future. Put down both needs and wants.

	NEEDS	WANTS
PERSONAL		
PROFESSIONAL		

STEP 2

Look at your needs column. What are the most important priorities personally and professionally? It is important that you only start out working on a few at a time. If you try to do everything at once, you will become overwhelmed and quit. Then, figure out the things you need to do to get those needs met.

STEP 3

Now go through your wants and do the same thing as Step 2 above. Don't overlook this. Part of having balance in life is having both your needs and wants met. Obviously, your needs are more important, but without the wants, you give up hope.

STEP 4

Set up a timeline for those needs to be accomplished. What are you going to do today, this week, this month, this year, and in the next five years to bring yourself to reach those priorities?

STEP 5

Do the same thing for your wants. Set up your timeline of completion.

STEP 6

DO THE ACTIONS. Here is where the rubber meets the road. You can plan and plan and plan, but if there is no action involved you will be in the same place, with the same problems, five years from now.

STEP 7

Re-evaluate. Every few months go back through this whole process again.

As you grow and change, so will your priorities, your needs and your wants.

THE BEST WAY TO ACCOMPLISH THIS

Very rarely can a person accomplish this alone. Have you ever heard the saying, "You can't see the forest for the trees?" That is what happens in our lives. We get so caught up in the unimportant things right in front of us, that we miss the big picture and we don't recognize growth when it occurs.

Now, you do have several options. One is to have family members try to help you through this. While you do need their support, they are usually looking at the same trees you are and can miss things.

Two, you can go to friends for help. They do tend to see more of the big picture, but many times they can't give you the encouragement and motivation you need at times to get past yourself.

Three, you work with a professional who knows how to help you bring balance to your life. They can come alongside of you and guide you to the quickest path to success because there will be obstacles that try to stop you. Did I forget to mention that?

No road to balance is smooth; little pebbles will get into your shoes to irritate you and take your focus off your goals. Barriers will be put up that you will have to learn how to go over, under, around or through. People will get in your way and tell you that it is the wrong road to take and you should follow them. All sorts of things will try to keep you from what you want.

Coaches are keen observers who can not only help you with what is going on right now, but they have been down your road and they know what is up ahead and can keep you moving forward, even when everything is telling you to stop.

That is what I'm offering to be for you. Let me help you on your path to balance in your life. I have been on both sides of the coin, and I can guide you through the roughest parts. I can relate to what you are feeling and am more than willing to help you navigate this wonderful thing called life.

First of all, if you would like more information on how to start this process, you can pre-order my upcoming book at www.dennisgarrido.com Second, you can email me at dennis@dennisgarrido.com and request your free 15-minute phone consultation where we can discuss your situation and see if we are a good fit for each other. Third, maybe you realize more people need to hear this message. I am also available to speak to groups and conferences. If so, just send me an email, and we can arrange a time to speak.

No matter what you decide, know this. You can achieve balance in your life. It is possible. I can tell you that it has been worth everything I went through to get to this point. The peace I experience now, compared to the chaos I lived before, is so amazing and I wish the same for you.

Don't miss out. Make the choice to change your life today, and I guarantee that you won't regret it!!!

www.ingramcontent.com/pod-product-compliance
Lightning Source LLC
Chambersburg PA
CBHW070752100426
42742CB00012B/2108